the ticket
life-changing journeys

Boise Valley
Christian Communion
Boise, Idaho

GOOD CATCH PUBLISHING

This book was written for the express purpose of conveying the love and mercy of Jesus Christ. The statements in this book are substantially true; however, names and minor details have been changed to protect people and situations from accusation or incrimination.

Cover Photo: Chris Barker

Cover Design: Barker Design Group

V1.1

Acknowledgements

This is a collaborative effort of dozens, who have joined together to compile the powerful book you are holding in your hands. While I cannot mention every individual who has played a part in this project, I want to mention a few who went the extra mile.

I am grateful, most of all, to those whose lives are recorded here. To those who told their stories, whether published or not, thank you for inviting us along on your journeys.

Ann Ralstin saw a vision, sensed a right timing, and challenged me to consider the possibility. Your unflagging encouragement has lifted me.

Scott Nelson gave pastoral oversight to this project and critical support at key moments. I will never forget the words, "We are a team, so what can I do?" Your love for our community infused me with a sense of purpose.

All those who conducted interviews: Letty Barnes, Bob Holsclaw, Judy Holsclaw, Grace Ruddy, Cliff Seusy, Steve Sherer and Kathryn Wells. Your sensitivity and willingness to gently probe the storytellers' lives made this possible.

The writers who viewed life from the storytellers' vantage point, and ultimately made these stories your own: Marilyn Davis, Barb DeMoney-Smith, Karl Fritz, Pat Fujii, Eric Gironda, Judy Holsclaw, Nola McCafferty,

Brenda Nelson, Kathy Pipal, Debbie Roam, Richard Russell, John Seibold and Shelly Williams. You gave words to the often unimaginable and, without you, there would be no finish line.

The editors who walked the fine line between what works and what doesn't: Steve Reames, Candace van Hout and Kathryn Wells. You are a brave lot.

The team leaders: Bobbie Hobson, Vicki Robertson, Candace van Hout, Kathryn Wells and Rachel Wilson, along with their faithful proofreaders, worked tirelessly. Your attention to detail was refreshingly keen.

The Inside Out team generated cover ideas, and Donna Barker took the foggy vision for a book cover and made it reality. Christopher Barker's photography and color manipulation added the final punch we were looking for.

Julie Penn, our publishing consultant, lent a much-needed critical eye and wise direction. Your boundless encouragement hit the mark and kept me focused.

Don Anderson, my husband and champion: your sense of humor rescued me repeatedly during this project. When you shouldered the most important jobs that no one else saw, I noticed.

Finally, to those special people who never tired of the intensity of this work, especially Ginger, and my

Acknowledgements

Tuesday friends, who went above and beyond the call of friendship. Your selflessness made all the difference.

Cindy Anderson,
Project Manager

Special Thanks

When undertaking a project of this magnitude, there will always be some people who project vision, and those who turn visions into realities. Cindy Anderson has acknowledged many of those involved in this project, which deserve thanks. However, had it not been for Cindy, this book would have remained only a dream. She took the idea, then mobilized volunteers and trained people who never dreamed they would be a part of something as significant as this book. Thank you, Cindy, on behalf of a grateful congregation and on behalf of those who will ultimately read these stories and gain the hope that their lives can change, too. Cindy's husband, Don, and her family have also been a great help through their encouragement and sacrifice over the past five months.

Pastor Scott Nelson is most deserving of thanks for the hours of time he invested during the production of this book. He has conferred with Cindy and the book team numerous times, and has served as a great encouragement to them.

Thanks to the congregation, and especially the ones who humbly told the stories that make up this book. They are the ones who have exemplified the truth of redemption time and again over the years. These grace-filled people genuinely live life in gratitude for all God has done for them.

Finally, had it not been for my wife, Ann, there would likely never have been a book. She heard Daren Lindley of Good Catch Publishing share his passion to get significant stories into print, and show others that there is, indeed, hope for them. Ann not only knew that we needed to do the book project, but she knew Cindy Anderson was the one who could do the project and make it a reality. She took the information from Daren, gave it to Cindy, projected the vision of what it could mean to the congregation and this book was born. Thank you, Ann, for looking ahead and seeing things that are not, as though they are! We are all blessed by your vision and enthusiasm.

Montie Ralstin,
Lead Pastor

Contents

Introduction

We all love a good story. This is a book filled with great stories. I enjoy reading *Outdoor Life* whenever I have the time. Its monthly article entitled "This Happened to Me!" contains harrowing true tales of people who have survived life-threatening, outdoor adventures. The book you are holding has some of the most important this-happened-to-me stories of our day because they are the real life adversities the people of our community have faced head on and overcome. These are not tame stories, and as you read, perhaps you'll find similarities with your own life.

Life is often difficult or seems terribly unfair in comparison to others. Our lives might differ somewhat from these; nevertheless, these stories are true. Yet, they represent just a fraction of the life experiences around us every day. These people have chosen to tell their stories in a public arena. They are not trying to call attention to themselves nor elevate the often horrific circumstances they found themselves in, whether by choice or by force. Rather, they tell stories to reveal the redemptive work in their lives, as they were delivered from their circumstances. They live life today out of what they have learned from their past, and they live it with great hope for their future.

I know all of these people and some I know very well, having walked with them through some of their life's journey. They are genuine, transformed, humble and grateful. Most of all, they are still in the process of learning to live this transformed life. I admire their tenacity and courage, and you will too. So grab your favorite beverage, curl up in a comfortable chair and go with them on their incredible journeys.

Chapter 1
Blindsided

The Story of Wes Newell

"Get me off the boat, not off the planet," Corey hinted.

I flinched as Corey gave me technical instructions. He had downloaded anatomy books and practiced shooting things with the same density as bone.

"You have to do this," Corey insisted. "I can't hold the gun steady enough and maintain the correct angle." He planned to shoot himself, even if I refused to help him.

As he lay on the grass, I pressed the barrel of the gun directly against his shoulder. We couldn't risk either one of us flinching. It could mess up the plan for a clean exit wound.

I pulled the trigger. Inadvertently, I stepped back and waited. Corey didn't move. As it had so often before, my life spun crazily out of control. I was no stranger to violence.

As a kid, my mother's bizarre patterns were familiar, and I was fully aware for years that she used drugs almost continuously. From time to time, she sobered up and threw all the drugs out of the house, except for the stash my step dad, Bill, refused to give up. Then she'd drag my brother and me to church, to show the world how respectable and clean she was.

Clap-clap. Clap. Louder. I resented her hypocrisy.

Clap-clap-clap. Louder. Louder. At eleven years

old, I did everything to make trouble, even in the front row during the church service. I could make enormous noise purposely clapping offbeat during the music. Brent, who was a year younger than I, started snickering when people looked my way.

When we arrived home, my mother slammed the car door, marched me across the driveway and shoved me through the front door of the house.

"Bill!" she shouted. "Bill, you will not believe how embarrassed I am."

"Huh?" Bill was slouched in front of the TV and obviously irritated. After a minute of listening to my mother screaming, he grabbed Brent and me by the arm and dragged us to the spare bedroom where he beat us both.

Even ten years later, alone in prison, anger surged in me as I replayed those beatings. The worst part was seeing Brent abused. I hated watching, feeling helpless. I swore I'd stand up to any injustice I could. And I'd NEVER be like my mother.

At least that was true about drugs. I never touched them. I didn't need those kinds of chemicals to brighten my life. My friends and I enjoyed other means of entertainment all through high school. By then, I was old enough to quit participating in the church charade.

"Hey, Brad," I said, through the open window of my Mustang.

Brad leaned the passenger seat forward, squishing Corey's face into the dashboard.

"Knock it off, you piece of...." Laughter and a slug in the arm greeted him as he plopped down next to his comrades. We bobbed our heads in unison to the music streaming from the cassette deck.

"How many have you gotten so far?"

"We lost count an hour ago, you dip," I replied as I pulled away from the curb.

"Hand me a slingshot." Brad pulled a handful of steel balls from his pocket.

The next day's paper told the whole story: "Vandal spree costs valley residents thousands in broken glass..." January 25, 1987.

It didn't take long until the newspaper became a public diary of our activities. It wasn't that I had too much time on my hands because I was working forty hours a week besides going to high school. It was just a pleasure to tick people off. One of the days I wasn't working after school, Brad came over to work on our latest project. He let himself in, banging the doorknob into the wall.

"Watch the wall. I'm the one who has to patch that, you puke." Brad stepped behind me to look over my shoulder. We had pooled our money and bought a ready-made pipe bomb. A wooden crate, emptied of an old RCA phonograph, was coughing up its guts to make room to stow the new device for safekeeping.

"Did you get it?" Brad couldn't hide his anticipation.

"What do you think that is?"

"Cool!" he examined the weighty tubular device. It wasn't like he could see anything inside the seal of the smooth metal shell.

"We'll save a lot of money on the next one." I closed the lid on the box after placing the bomb inside. "I watched him put this together. It's no big deal. We can get the parts all right." The date of birth on my fake ID cast me as a 21-year-old, old enough to buy explosives for our nighttime raids on a deserving target's mailbox.

Later that night, we paced off the distance of four front yards, four driveways, and four mailboxes to the target. We paused, lit the match and ignited a three-foot fuse to the door of the mailbox. The explosion occurred after we were a safe distance away, laughing and catching our breath.

Two days later, I flipped to the local section of the Idaho Statesman to see how they chronicled our latest activities: ". . . in a sporadic, month-long streak of terror, local high school principal loses five mailboxes to vandals. . ." February 15, 1987.

After the first one, blowing things up became sort of a trademark. If I didn't like a neighbor, I would leave bombs on his windowsill. Bombs also worked nicely on cars. Somehow I never got caught. Not that the police didn't suspect me, I just never had the equipment when they came to the house.

"Shut up and hand me the fuse." I motioned impatiently toward the waterproof fuse. The stall door kept swinging shut, providing with each tap a tense moment, just the right threshold of added risk.

"That makes a lot of noise. We're going to get caught."

"No way, Clay has the hallway covered." Echoes seemed to travel to infinity in a grid of tile floors and brick walls. Although we had almost four years of experience with blowing things up by now, this was our first job in a building, much less a school. Jeremy, a fellow student, came through the bathroom door unexpectedly.

"What's that smell? Who did that one?" The pungent odor of sulfur was one of the milder hazards that

20

Blindsided

Jeremy had walked in on. I sensed a snitch was brewing. Although I only weighed 125 pounds, my reputation for revenge intimidated the 185-pound Jeremy.

"What are you guys doing? School's closed. How did you get in here? What's that smell?"

I handed the sulfur bomb to my accomplice behind the stall door and stepped around to approach the intruder.

One of my buddies, Tucker, took the fall out of loyalty, and the rest of us escaped punishment. This time the article read: "One boy being expelled from local high school apparently coincides with the end of a four-year reign of terror. . . " October 21, 1990.

My escape from Idaho was scheduled with the Navy recruiter a year following graduation. Grades notwithstanding, the requirements for acquiring the needed diploma were loosely fulfilled within the appointed time. Fred, my biological dad, provided moral support and a room after my mother vanished under the haze of a long cocaine binge.

Boot camp gave me a whole new environment and I made a deliberate decision to get to know God. I developed a habit of prayer and Bible study. I didn't even mind when others nicknamed me "The Reverend." But it was an odd feeling when my shipmates started dropping their moral dilemmas into conversations. Some even outright asked for my advice. *Man, you are asking the wrong guy,* I thought. *If you only knew.*

In boot camp, I started earning respect in a different way. Instead of being the instigator of chaos and destruction, I set out to achieve perfection where the military was concerned. Graduating at the top of my class, I earned letters of commendation. Things were clicking together for the first time in my life. I was making friends and a few of us ended up being stationed on the same ship. One of my buddies, Matt, shared my aspirations. He had hopes of becoming a Navy Seal. Matt was probably one of the most intelligent people I had ever met. But he never got the peer approval he needed to make Navy Seal.

Matt had the misfortune of being the victim of unfounded rumors that he was homosexual, which stemmed from a whimsical decision to color his own hair black. In the midst of President Clinton's political handling of the issue of gays in the military, he should have avoided provoking his fellow seamen. For Matt, once the gates of persecution were opened, the dam burst with a vengeance. Echoes from my life of being a super-protector for my younger brother gave me resolve. I refused to abandon my friend.

For almost a year, I watched Matt suffer unjustly. Every bit of extra detail was thrown at him. He was ridiculed and demeaned publicly by the Petty Officer. When we tried out for the Search and Rescue team, Matt and I were once again at the top. They told us they were going to send us out, but they hated Matt, and since they categorized me with him, we never got to go. Instead, the threats of violence against Matt intensified.

One night, I returned to our ship after an evening of shore leave. The stars became invisible, and I gazed, not at the heavens, but at the reflection of the ship's many lights from the upper three decks. Dangling my legs off the steel hull six stories above the lapping waves below, I started talking to God.

"God, I thought that you were with me. Matt needs you and you're abandoning him. If you're not going to step in and give us some help through this, then I don't want anything to do with you." From that moment on, I simply walked away from God. I decided to take matters into my own hands. After seeing Matt's treatment, I thought we should run up the chain of command. When I called the special sexual harassment hotline, I got promises.

"These types of allegations warrant an investigation," the Captain assured me. "I will definitely look into this." The only result, though, was that my phone call evoked stiffer persecution and the ire of the ship's Commanding Officer. The threats climaxed when Matt discovered a carefully planted newspaper article describing a spree of beatings against gay men, with headlines circled in ink. The implications were plain: All fags must die. This meant there would be all-out war on the ship.

While we were in port, I developed a habit of hanging out with my friend, Corey, who had an apartment in San Diego. I met Corey when he was assigned to our ship while we were docked in Florida for repairs. Corey and I hit it off right away. We figured out we knew some of the same people, and the three of us, including Matt, became pretty good friends.

Corey had entered the military on a medical waiver. He had tinnitus, which made loud noises painful for him. He was supposed to be in a zero free noise environment. It was ridiculous that he was even on my ship. An aircraft carrier is about one of the noisiest environments on the planet.

Just like I did with Matt, I fought hard to help Corey work through the red tape that was forcing him to work in this impossible situation. The Commanding Officer overrode the doctor's findings to force Corey to remain aboard. The findings of a second and a third physician were also rejected. Our CO spitefully ignored my pleadings and those of the other shipmates as well.

The only relief was that when we were in dock, Corey could get off the ship since he lived in San Diego. At Corey's apartment one night, I continued operating as a crusader of the defenseless.

"Hey, Karla, why did Corey head up to the apartment so soon?" I was left in the hot tub with Corey's girlfriend, Karla, her friend, and a neighbor gal.

"I think he was just tired and wanted to hit the sack," Karla replied.

Although there were only three of us enjoying the relaxing bubbles, there were others celebrating in the courtyard, growing louder and more raucous with every alcoholic beverage consumed. It wasn't too long before a few Marines took notice of the bathing beauties accompanying me in the hot tub. One Marine brazenly started grabbing Karla's neighbor.

"Come over here, and I'll give you a Christmas present," slurred the belligerent marauder.

"Get your filthy hands off me," her voice rose with fear. "Don't touch me!"

"Hey! Did you hear the lady? She said don't touch her," I spoke up, aware that she was pretty defenseless against the mob that had taken notice and was quickly approaching.

"Why don't you shut your mouth before I drown you," the Marine snarled as he grabbed for me to hold me under.

I quickly jumped out of the water, knowing I was at an even greater disadvantage in the hot tub. I ran straight at the first brawny man and kicked him directly in the chest to put him down quickly.

Blindsided

More Marines streamed toward us. I fended for myself, alone. Karla did what she could by jumping on one of the aggressor's backs and throwing beer in the faces of others, but we were no match for the horde. White jacket sleeves wrapped around my chest from behind. There were at least twenty people in the crowd, making it impossible to tell whom I was fighting, and who was helping. After I was beaten pretty badly, the mob gradually dissipated at the violent urging of Karla and two female neighbors.

A six-foot, metal lamppost lay on the concrete path next to me. The mixture of adrenaline and pain had caused me to draw upon brute survival rage, and the unfulfilled plans of an eleven-year-old boy murdering his cruel stepfather with a baseball bat. At the edge of the pool, I swung that lamppost, hitting a Marine with a wicked blow. I had pulled the post from its place with my bare hands.

I blinked at the full moon as my rib cage rocked against the ground and the last departing Marine booted my side gut. The next thing I heard were voices, as someone prepped me for surgery in the emergency room.

"I can't do this," I heard a man's voice say. I tried to see what the commotion was about, but all I could see was the doctor's head shaking. I couldn't see my right hand because of the blue, cloth curtain erected across my torso. A tourniquet-like device was attached to my upper arm to prevent the loss of additional blood.

"Who's the hand guy from Scripps Memorial? This is unreal. Call him and get him out of bed. We can't fix this."

I tried to understand the words that were coming from the doctor in front of me. "Crenshaw is the specialist on call. He'll be here in an hour." It took four hours to place the splintered bones back under the skin, without general anesthesia. Shock and trauma were the only barriers between any sense of pain and shredded ligaments that lay in the open air.

Subconsciously, I continued to fulfill my vow: Don't look to God for any help. Rebuilding hand muscles that had atrophied for weeks and working taut replacement tissue was grueling. I felt it an act of valor to recover quicker than anyone expected. During physical therapy, I was given Temporary Assigned Duty in naval office facilities, since I couldn't crawl on the ladders where I usually worked. It was a remarkably better environment. Generally, when we were in port, there was less tension, as some of the guys had duties off the boat. It was when we pulled out to sea, and the men were away from their families, that life became more hostile.

The U.S.S. Constellation was scheduled to depart and Matt made up his mind he wouldn't be aboard. The week before the ship was to leave, Matt's desperation mounted.

"If you break my leg, I won't have to get on that ship," he said for the hundredth time. I couldn't stand it—day after day, he hounded me. "I want you to drive over my leg with the car."

"You're crazy!" I argued. "Get a grip on reality."

"Wes, if I go to sea, I won't come back alive. I'm not getting on that ship." Threats against Matt had escalated even off the ship. One guy threatened to cut Matt's throat if he even saw him around town.

"I'm going to set myself on fire, Wes." I knew he wasn't joking. "I'll do it right in front of the ship. I'd rather make my point now, instead of waiting for some-

26

one to kill me onboard."

I knew he was going to take his own life, and I couldn't stand by and see that happen. We went to Home Depot and bought a steel pipe. Somehow I drifted from being a confidant to an accomplice.

Matt chose a location within a two-minute drive to the Balboa Naval Medical Center along Balboa Avenue. Leaning against the car, he instructed me, "Break the fibula, it's a smaller bone and will heal faster."

I took a golf swing at Matt's calf, eight inches above the ankle. Thud. Matt groaned in pain and started jumping around.

"Dude, this is crazy. I'm not doing this," I said as I got back into the car.

"Leave me then. I'll stay and do something myself." His tone left no doubt as to his intentions.

In a dreamlike mode, I made a second attempt. It was surreal. Finally, on the third try came the anticipated yielding of flesh with a muffled snap.

Feeling horror and relief, I drove him to the hospital. As we had planned, I reinforced his made-up story of being jumped for his military ID, which was a hot enough item to warrant being mugged.

As quickly as I could, I returned to Corey's apartment. I knew he wouldn't be there. He had taken a vacation, knowing we would have to pull out soon. Right after I got back to the apartment, however, Corey showed up. He had just driven twenty-two hours straight, pulled up to the apartment, got his gun out and was ready to go right then.

"Will you drive me to the hospital?"

"No, dude, you can't do this." I couldn't believe this was happening twice in one day. He didn't know about Matt, so I told him. That seemed to make everything he was proposing more viable. I followed him in my own car to the park.

It was easier to shoot Corey than it had been to break Matt's leg. After I shot him, I thought he was dead. He didn't move. It was like he was frozen, or maybe I was, or maybe time itself was frozen. I started panicking when I realized that Corey was not moving.

After a few seconds of eternity, he opened his eyes with a low moan. "Holy crap!" Corey yelled. The muzzle burns were invisible in the darkness as Corey got to his feet and faced away so I could check for the exit wound.

Corey moved gingerly in the direction of his car where he had left the driver's door open. He could make it to the hospital without assistance. I followed at a distance and watched across the hospital parking lot until Corey reached the emergency room's automatic doors.

Back at the apartment, the phone rang. It was Matt.

"Dude, you're not gonna believe this."

"Try me," I said pretty innocently.

"Corey just came in to emergency. He was shot."

The stories started to fall apart right away. The San Diego police were immediately suspicious of Matt's story, which conjured absurd visions of a gang of malevolent ankle beaters. Corey claimed that he was attacked and shot in a skirmish at point-blank range, but doctors saw a "miracle shot" that skirted any hint of a vital organ. It was too coincidental. These guys knew each other and were admitted hours apart.

NCIS charged Corey and Matt with malingering, and fueled a full-scale investigation that was directly initiated by the Commanding Officer of the U.S.S. Constellation. It was his chance to get even.

The court martial drew national media coverage. The best lawyers in the country offered their services, pro bono. Our lawyer, Doug, was eminently known nationwide. He immediately began working on a duress defense, believing that all three of us had solid cases and would be found innocent. Doug agreed that I could not, in good conscience, have permitted my buddies to end their lives without intervention. Even some of the jurors told me, "You're never going to be convicted." It seemed everyone felt I was innocent.

While the pressure of national politics and media exposure mounted, I stood my ground. *God, how can I ask you to help me when I was the one who walked away from you?*

Fortunately, I ended up with a special court martial, rather than a general court martial. After I was pronounced guilty, I was sentenced to three months in the brig, and was released two weeks early for good behavior.

Back home in Idaho, I needed companionship, but recoiled from the potential for another hurtful relationship. An insidious and spiteful bitterness was rooting itself in me, and fed off my isolation.

I kept in touch with Matt and Corey. They had both been released honorably, and we had many conversations.

"I know I've said this a million times, Wes, but you probably saved my life," Matt said as consolation.

"Yeah. Don't mention it."

"Wes, I'm the luckiest guy in the world to have a friend like you. I don't know if I could have done what you did," Matt reminded me.

His appreciation wasn't anything to me. I knew my own motives. *I was the one who turned my back on God. How could I expect him to want to have anything to do with me?* The concept I could never grasp was forgiveness. I didn't really know God, and I didn't know what lengths he would go to for me.

One day I met a girl. As we talked, she asked, "Were you ever at a hockey game? Saying stuff to this person?"

Oh my gosh, I called this girl every name you can think of. I remembered the hockey game where I was totally drunk. I had just broken up with my girlfriend, and I yelled at her all the way across the hockey rink. As things progressed, we started to hang out and she ended up forgiving me for my extreme rudeness. It began to open my eyes to the whole concept of forgiveness.

I dated this girl who forgave me, and thought, *Wow, this girl might be the one. I can't believe this!*

Driving down the road one day, I had this intense feeling, like a voice inside me saying: *I gotta get my butt back to church.* It was good for me, but my girlfriend couldn't handle a real change in me.

"So first you're like this person—now you're this other person. I don't want anything to do with you. You're crazy!" I tried to talk to her, even tried to pray with her, but she was adamant. "You're crazy, you're totally crazy. I don't want to have anything to do with you."

That day I flipped my Bible open and read out loud: "My dear brothers and sisters, if anyone among you wanders away from the truth and is brought back again, you can be sure that the one who brings that person back will save that sinner from death and bring about the forgiveness of many sins." James 5:19

I totally melted. Here I was, a grown man, bawling in my room. I had never experienced anything like this. *Forgiveness is real. God says he'll take me back even though I rejected him.* For the first time, I understood forgiveness and how much God loved me. For a man who had been flung about within loose boundaries for thirty years, it seemed appropriate that a mighty relief would emerge through no workings of my own. I was blindsided by this love. I believed my rejection of God was final and irrevocable. But God had not accepted my refusal. The mercy and forgiveness that had been squashed from my life at such an early age became animated and abundant.

As I read the verse again and again, it confirmed that forgiveness was real. It belonged to me.

Chapter 2
All the Wrong Places
The Story of Betty West

I knocked on the door and waited.

"Come in, we are very glad you're here," the stranger said, as he opened the door. I followed him into a room so dark it was difficult to see where I was going. The light from a single candle and an unfamiliar scent tickled my senses. As my eyes adjusted, I saw eight or ten other people seated around the room. "Have a seat," the leader said, as he handed me a small slip of paper and a pen. "We are here to have our questions answered by someone who has passed through the veil of death to the other side. Write your questions on this slip of paper, and we will contact someone over there to answer them," he instructed.

I came to the séance out of curiosity. The untimely deaths of my aunt and uncle gave me another reason to seek the unknown. I wrote my question to them, and dropped the slip of paper into the hat circulating around the room. I waited as questions were drawn, read, and apparently answered by someone from the other side. As my question was drawn, my skin prickled with a strange sense of foreboding. I knew it was my question before the leader read it.

"How is it over there?" The leader asked my question to the one on the other side. A force I had never experienced before, and could not explain, hit me. I felt as if someone had punched me. It distracted me so much that

I didn't hear the answer to my question. I had contacted a power beyond this world, and in so doing, I began a journey of enticement and deception that would continue for many years.

My attraction to supernatural things began years earlier in a Chicago apartment, where I lived as an only child with my mother and father. My early life was easy in many ways since my mother stayed at home. Most of the time, my father was either absent, or very busy and distracted with his work. Although my family did not attend church, and didn't speak about God in our home, my parents permitted me to go to church with my friend's family.

"Your uncle is coming to live with us for a while," my mom announced one day. "Your father has found him a job here." My mother's brothers lived with us for brief periods of time during the Depression when jobs were hard to come by. I loved those times. The adults regularly gathered on Sunday mornings, in their bathrobes, around the breakfast table to discuss and argue politics and religion. I tried to remain quiet and appear invisible so I could stay and listen to what they were saying. Someone always took the role of devil's advocate. They punctuated these conversations by pounding their fists on the table, and voicing loud disagreements. These arguments were my primary early religious education.

During my childhood, most people used coal to heat their homes and the snow was usually blackened with soot. One evening, when I was ten years old, a winter storm dropped fresh white powder snow, not yet coated with soot. From a velvety evening sky, brilliant stars reflected their light on the glistening snow below. The beauty of the scene filled me with such excitement

34

that I spun around and jumped into the air, clicking my heels together. For the first time in my life, I knew there was a wonderful God who had created such beauty. I longed to know this God, but I had no idea how to find him.

"Betty, come with me to church camp this summer," my friend begged. "We'll have a wonderful time." Church camp was a new and exciting experience for me until the final evening. All the teens sat in a circle, around a blazing fire, and shared stories about how Jesus had made a difference in their lives.

"Jesus is great," a shy, redheaded girl said. "He's like a friend who never leaves me alone."

"Yeah, he loves me no matter what," a boy answered.

Following the campfire, many of them sneaked behind the bushes to smoke cigarettes and make out. Since I didn't do those things, I thought—*if this is Christianity, I don't want any part of it.*

I moved to Phoenix during my senior year in high school. Within a couple of years, I was married with three little girls. Needing to escape the Arizona heat, my husband and I moved our young family to Lewiston, Idaho. There we had a son, and I managed a motel in addition to caring for four small children. I was soon overwhelmed, however, and escaped the pressure by enrolling in the local two-year college.

College was the highlight of my week. I became involved in drama, finding friends among students who were free-thinking, New Age intellectuals. It was natural to adopt the arrogant and self-centered attitudes of my friends. My cynicism drew me to reincarnation, astrology, numerology, positive thinking, and various other metaphysical subjects. I bought expensive books and read for hours. Through my study, I became a sincere believer in all these things, priding myself on having an inquisitive mind. I was a seeker. It was my desire to know the unknown that finally led me to attend the séance.

One day, a man entered the motel and approached the counter. "May I help you?" I asked, expecting him to request a room.

"Are you saved?" he asked. I stood there unable to answer. A question flashed through my mind. *Saved? For what? From what?* I don't remember how I answered the man, but my attitude clearly expressed the arrogance and cynicism deep inside me.

After six years in Idaho, we moved our family to Seattle, and my husband resumed working in construction. Each weekend we worked on remodeling our own home. I continued to research the occult and study the books I had acquired in Lewiston.

"What happened to you?" I asked my daughter in alarm one day. I came home to find her lying down with a huge lump and bruise on her forehead.

"I got hit with a baseball bat," she answered. I prayed over her using phrases I had learned from my metaphysical research. The lump went down. This increased my conviction that there was power in these beliefs. Surely they could not fail.

But then the bombshell dropped.

"You must have surgery," the doctor told me. "You have a tumor on your aorta. It is affecting the autonomic nervous system and there will be multiple tumors. This is very serious."

I postponed surgery, believing that the power of positive thinking and the metaphysical principle of

All the Wrong Places

"mind over matter" would heal me as it had healed my daughter. While I went through various mental calis-thenics and positive thinking exercises, the tumor grew to the size of a small pear, putting pressure on my aorta, esophagus and lung. Any excitement caused me to lose my breath. I grew increasingly disappointed and doubtful as I realized that what I believed was not working. After two years, I finally scheduled the surgery.

Four years after we moved to Seattle, we sold our home and moved south to Medford, Oregon. We fol-lowed the familiar pattern of building a new home for our family. I decided that the children needed some religious training and joined Unity Church. Unity teaches reincar-nation and that Jesus is one of many masters. I soon be-came a teacher for the teenage class. We used the Bible, but considered it to be an allegory. The tenets of Unity were a good fit with my beliefs.

"I didn't see Mary this morning," I remarked one day to a mutual friend.

"Oh, didn't you know— she's not coming to meet-ings anymore. Mary said she was, um, disillusioned with Unity. She's not coming back."

Mary had left and didn't call me with an explana-tion, but that was not unusual. My friend was a quiet and discreet person who seldom called her friends.

A few weeks later, Mary called. "Hi, Betty, I've missed you."

"I've missed you, too, Mary. Are you okay?" I hon-estly wanted to know.

"I'm good. Really good. I'm meeting at my house with a few other women. I'd like it if you could join us." She said they were going to discuss a recorded talk by Bill Bright, the founder of an organization called Campus

Crusade for Christ. I had never heard of Bill Bright, but I went to the meeting to see Mary. Mr. Bright talked about the Four Spiritual Laws, and explained how to find God through knowing Jesus.

I could not understand anything he said. I understood the idea of working to gain favor with God. I understood being personally responsible for my own wrongdoings. But I could not understand why anyone, especially Jesus, would do the work for me and die to pay for my sins. As I left Mary's house that day I thought, *well, they certainly were lovely ladies, but they really need to be enlightened.*

Building our home in Medford was a long and tedious process. After working all day, my husband continued to work in his shop until bedtime. It was a busy and frustrating time for me, but my childhood desire to know God was renewed. I had never really quit searching for God—I was just looking for him in all the wrong places.

"Betty," my husband said, "we need some more building supplies. Please run to the lumberyard for me. Here's a list."

"Sure. I'll do it right now. I'm on my way out anyway." Several times a week, I went on errands to buy building materials for our home. Near the completion of the project, my hunger to find God increased. As I ran errands, I started searching for a church that was open so I could go in and pray. Many times I stopped at churches only to find their doors locked. Frustrated, and feeling more desperate in my search to know God, I kept looking. On my way to the lumberyard one day, I spotted a large church with a steeple. Slamming on the brakes, I squealed into the parking lot.

I tried the door and it opened. Light streamed

through the colored, stained glass windows, making patterns on the floor and dimly lighting the interior of the church. Statues, near the front, stood at attention like soldiers. A large cross bearing a dying Jesus hung on the front wall of the church. It seemed to draw me closer. I moved forward, sat in a pew, and stared at the cross in front of me. I didn't know how to pray, but simply said, "God, you've got to reveal yourself to me." As I repeated this prayer over and over, I sensed someone in the room with me. I peeked through squinted eyes expecting to see angels, but I didn't see angels or anyone else. Instead, I felt love and peace pouring through my body like warm oil. It felt so good, I wanted to stay there forever. For the next three months, I returned to this church two or three times a week, always praying the same prayer, "God, please reveal yourself to me."

We were putting the final touches on our new home. My daughter and I painted the entire inside of the house. All that remained to paint was the woodwork.

"Dear, I want to hire someone to finish painting. I am tired of painting and I don't cut in well. I really don't want to paint the woodwork," I appealed to my husband.

"Sure. Call around and see who is available." We hired a part-time painter who was also the pastor of a local church. As he painted the woodwork, he sang Christian songs. He was the happiest person I had met in a long time. *Was God answering my prayers?* I wondered. Maybe he was revealing himself to me. I determined to visit the church more often in the coming days.

I had been disenchanted with Unity for some time. Compared to what I was experiencing at the Catholic Church, Unity seemed dead and stale. I was tired of pale substitutes. I wanted God. So, like my friend, Mary, I left the Unity Church.

Finally, the house was finished and we were moving in the last of our things. I sat in the middle of my kitchen floor surrounded by paper and boxes. *What's this?* I thought, removing a casserole pan from the debris. *Oh, I remember, Mary left this pan at my home following the youth potluck dinner several months ago.* The following day, I was running errands and decided to drop off the pan at Mary's house. When she answered the door, I handed her the pan and blurted out, "Mary, if you don't have the Holy Spirit, you don't have anything." I didn't know why I had said that, since I had no idea who or what the Holy Spirit was.

Tears filled Mary's eyes as she enveloped me in a hug. "Come in, Betty, and let me tell you." Mary shared her story with me that day.

"Betty, a few months ago when I left Unity, I was desperately seeking God, as you are now. A friend told me about Jesus and the simplicity of the gospel. She prayed with me and I asked Jesus into my life. I asked him to forgive me for my sins and to change me. I was so tired of trying to be perfect through my own efforts because it never worked." Mary went on to tell me that when she prayed, Christ gave her a new beginning and filled her with his Holy Spirit.

That's exactly what I had said when I came to her door, I thought.

"May I pray for you, Betty?" she asked.

As she prayed, the same peace and warmth that I experienced when I visited the church flowed over me. Mary sent a book home with me. I could hardly wait to read it because I anticipated that God would finally reveal himself to me through it.

All the Wrong Places

At last everyone is asleep. I breathed a weary sigh. The house was unusually quiet as I settled into my chair with a cup of tea and Mary's book. The book was easy to read and quite short. I quickly finished it, praying as I read. Somehow I knew that I must begin to yield my life to Jesus Christ.

"Jesus, I yield myself to you. Help me to know you," I prayed. Instantly, my teeth started grinding. My tongue and jaws began making strange movements, as if they had a will separate from mine. Inside me, the struggle accelerated between God and the evil spirit I had allowed into my life, through my intellectualism and pride.

Suddenly, I saw a picture in my mind of a theater marquee with the words: "Jacob Wrestling with the Angel." A few weeks before I quit Unity, I taught my teenaged class that Bible story. Jacob refused to let go of the angel until God blessed him. Remembering this story gave me the courage and strength to persist in yielding my life to Jesus.

Once again, I prayed, "Lord, I yield my life to you." I felt the evil spirit travel through my body, down my legs, and out through the bottom of my feet. As it left, I felt a heavy burden, like a huge weight, lift off me. My teeth stopped grinding and my jaws and tongue relaxed. I was free.

Immediately, another picture entered my mind. I saw the same theater marquee, but the words had changed. The bright, red letters spelled: PRIDE. I felt as if a blindfold had been removed from my eyes and I saw my problem clearly: pursuing intellectualism and occult vanities had filled me with pride. Pride, in turn, kept me from God all these years. Tears fell like rain as I prayed, "Lord, thank you for revealing yourself to me. Please forgive me and come into my life as my Lord and Savior."

Three days later, Mary called again to invite me to a meeting with some members of the Full Gospel Businessmen's organization and their wives. As they prayed for me, I was filled with the Holy Spirit. I wept, I laughed and I rejoiced. My search was over—I had found God. My empty searching in all the wrong places ended. He had revealed himself to me.

Within six months, all my family members asked Jesus into their lives. My children and I burned all the occult books I had once cherished to prevent anyone else from being trapped by the lies contained in them. I started praying with others who had become as disenchanted with metaphysics as I had been. When these seekers accepted Jesus, God gave them the same freedom I had found.

In my first juvenile disappointment in Christianity at camp, I was looking for perfection in people. I hadn't realized that, only in a relationship with Jesus, would I find true satisfaction. I am only complete in Christ. Now I look back and see that, all through my life, God was answering my prayer: Reveal yourself to me.

Chapter 3
Elusive Love
The Story of Jim and Letty Barnes

Jim raced the car's engine, ignoring the spinning wheels, as the car sped recklessly through town. It was a familiar scene. He was so angry and frustrated with Letty, she never seemed satisfied. Their regular arguments left Jim feeling enraged and this morning had been no exception.

"We need to get out of this town!" Letty's frustration erupted.

"We've been over this before, Letty, where in the world do you think we would go?" Jim asked as he finished knotting his tie.

"I don't care! Anywhere is better than here. I can't take another day of this. I hate this town. I hate this house. I hate our life." She felt the sting of tears blur her vision. "Please, Jim, can't we just start over somewhere else?"

Ignoring her pleas, he headed for the door. "Well, I can't talk about this right now." Jim's reply did nothing to settle her. "I have to get to work."

Her response was quick. "You don't care about us!"

The children, Nancy and Glenn, watched with wide eyes as their dad slammed the front door hard enough to rattle the windows. Several mornings a week he drove around town for almost half an hour. His anger was out of control; he needed the time to cool down to face a day of work. As he slowed the car, the memories of the morning cascaded down, some to remember and others to forget.

Jim and Letty had grown up in Enid, Oklahoma, where their families were longtime friends. Jim knew Letty as the baby sister of his best friend, Ted. When they married in 1961, they were not head over heels in love, though they did have a lot in common and had mutual respect for one another. Marriage appeared to be the next natural step for their relationship.

But Letty's life had not been a series of natural steps at all. Her senior year of college had been the roughest of her life. Her mother, while fighting breast cancer, received a blood transfusion that was contaminated with hepatitis, and she died as a result of it.

Letty, now engaged, wanted more than anything to have her mother there to help plan her wedding. *Oh, I can't take the pain of this.* Letty fought through tears. She wanted to be strong for her father and brother, though being the baby, she wasn't accustomed to being the rock of the family. While juggling the demands of school, she tried to give support to her dad. Letty exhausted herself flying back and forth from college. Though she was weary, she continued to plan her wedding, missing her mother's presence every step of the way. *I wonder how much of this I can take? I can't believe I'm going from planning a funeral, to planning a wedding.* Near the end of the school year, Letty received a call from her brother, who was away at graduate school.

"Letty, how are you?" Ted asked. She sensed that this wasn't a call about her wellbeing. She had been back to her dorm less than a week after her last trip home.

44

"Fine," she answered. "What's wrong?" She was anxious to know why Ted was calling.

"Dad's had a heart attack, Letty." She gripped the phone booth with both hands, feeling as though her life was crashing down around her. "Can you go home? It's pretty bad."

"I'll leave as soon as I can." She hoped it would be soon enough.

"Take care of yourself and take care of Dad," Ted finished. As always, Letty's brother was a steadying force in her life.

C'mon, Dad, you can make it. Hold on, Dad. Letty wasn't much for praying, but if any thoughts could go out to her dad and make a difference, these surely would. Despite her pleas, deeper heartache awaited her. Just six weeks after losing her mother, Letty buried her father, too.

The usual joy of a wedding was lost in the face of Letty's despair. It felt as if the world had whirled off its axis and was spinning crazily out of control. Within five months Letty lost both of her parents, graduated from college, and got married.

Although Jim recognized that Letty was unhappy, he did not realize the depth of the depression and hopelessness she felt. For nine years of their marriage, Letty lived in a deep hole where no light could reach. Jim did not meet her emotional needs. During these troubled times, Letty desperately needed Jim's attention and solace to get her through her days. Feeling incapacitated, Letty was unable to give the praise and positive strokes Jim lived for. The heavy loneliness she felt almost crushed her. It drew a curtain around her that Jim could not break through. "Letty," Jim reached out to touch her shoulder, "what can I do?" She shuddered and pulled away, tucking the blanket firmly around her.

"I can't take it," Letty sobbed, facing the wall away from Jim. He tried to rub her back, hoping, wishing, for any way to connect with her. Letty moved further away to the very edge of the bed.

"I love you," Jim whispered, but she never heard it. In her anguish, Letty cried herself to sleep night after night.

Letty knew Jim struggled with the coldness of their marriage; although he had moments of tenderness, they were fleeting and usually melted into anger. Consequently, Jim threw himself headlong into his insurance business to escape his stormy home life. His need for affirmation was met in the community. After taking over the lucrative insurance business he had shared with his dad, Jim became a rising star outside of the home. He joined civic clubs, served with the United Way, and became a pillar of the community. Guarding and building his reputation drove him. His successes were his defense against what was happening at home.

In their fourth year of marriage, Jim and Letty adopted a daughter, Nancy, and two years later a son, whom they named Glenn. Despite the joy of the children, the pain remained and no one knew the hidden secret in Letty's heart. During the day, while Nancy and Glenn napped or played, Letty contemplated divorce. It was contrary to their upbringing. Both families believed in "sticking it out" for better or for worse, though Letty never dreamed it would be this bad.

Letty had good friends in Enid, yet there was just no escaping the pain of her loss. Everyday activities with well-meaning people only stirred up the pain when they offered comfort. *Escape. If I could just escape*, she thought.

Elusive Love

Then came the chance.

After Ted finished graduate school, he married and moved out of state. Eventually, he opened a business in Boise, Idaho. One afternoon, Ted and Letty visited by phone, and he invited her, again, to come to Idaho.

"Letty, you and Jim should really think about it," Ted encouraged. "The people in Idaho are so friendly; I think you'd like it here."

"I don't know, Ted. Jim would never leave his business," Letty responded, yet the urging continued.

"The two of you would love the mountains and fresh air. It could be a new beginning."

Her conversation with Ted motivated Letty to speak to Jim that evening. The thought of a new beginning, a new town, and living close to her brother, gave Letty a lift. *Wouldn't it be great to get away from all the bad memories?* Her thoughts drifted as she fantasized about the possibilities. To Letty, Idaho was a breath of hope.

In 1969, Jim, Letty and the children visited Ted for Christmas. Soon thereafter, Jim sold his insurance business, moved his family to Idaho, and opened up a new business. Away from his hectic schedule, he was free to enjoy the outdoors of Idaho and spend more time with Letty and the kids. This was a recipe for contentment.

The Stanley Basin, just over a hundred miles east of Boise, became a second home to Jim and Letty. Even the weather could not cloud Letty's happiness on those muddy trails. Nancy and Glenn squealed while Jim carried one child in his arms and the other on his back, as they hiked out through incessant rains during one of their camping trips in the White Cloud Mountains. The jagged teeth of the Sawtooth Mountains were a majestic background for their newfound life together.

Letty enjoyed the simple life and the outdoors, but most of all, she had Jim back, and her heart sang that night. Despite the fact that her family was soaked from the rain and had to huddle for warmth, Letty was deliriously happy.

"Jim," Letty whispered, "I can't imagine life without you." She shivered as Jim took her in his arms. It was a rare moment. Even though they got along better, they still lacked interaction and emotional intimacy.

Jim's new business was growing and demanded more of his time, leaving less time for weekend backpacking trips. In Enid, Jim had narrowly missed receiving the Businessman of the Year award. After that disappointment, he vowed that he would simply work harder.

The Idaho bliss lasted only a year. Old problems began to resurface, and their relationship slowly started crumbling again.

"Jim, we have to talk. What is happening to us?" Letty asked in a panicked voice. "We're drifting apart again. I'm feeling lost and isolated from you." Letty wanted desperately to save whatever they had together.

Jim looked up from his papers. "Not now, Letty," he sighed as he turned back to his task. Full of frustration, Jim wanted to take Letty by the arms and shake her. He wanted to shout, "Stop haranguing me!" but didn't, which added to his simmering anger.

Although Jim and Letty attended church, they had never sought out counseling. They never even considered it. With their relationship continuing to dissolve into cycles of frustration, anger and eruption, both were thinking of divorce. Since Ted had taken that route, ending the marriage seemed more permissible to Jim and

48

Letty than ever before.

The thought of losing Jim left Letty hollow. When she was alone, she wept deeply for the loss of his love. She remembered her mother declaring more than once, "You be nice to Jim. He's the best thing that's happened to you!" With her mother's voice perpetually in her mind, she lived, breathed and walked in the hope that, one day, Jim would remember the vibrant woman he once loved.

Looking for answers, Letty contacted her pastor to share her growing despair. She was unaware that Jim sought help on that same day. Turning to God, Jim prayed: "God, I have done everything I can to make this marriage work, but I have failed. I don't know if you ever get involved in the events of this world, but if you do, please heal our marriage."

Jim and Letty turned to God for strength and their lives started changing dramatically. They no longer needed to preoccupy themselves with external activities; they were far too busy with church activities. Focusing their energy at the First Presbyterian Church, their marital problems seemed to fade as their spirituality grew. Letty was fulfilled and content, something she hadn't felt in years. For six months, they were giddy on a natural high. To add to their happiness, Letty was able to conceive. Contrary to medical predictions, their family increased by two more daughters, Mary and Ann. In her contentment, Letty no longer needed the crutch of the weekend camping trips, and Jim's excitement about God temporarily compensated his cravings for receiving personal praise.

Still, certain issues remained unresolved. Jim now sought recognition by throwing himself into church activities and, once again, lost focus on the marriage. He no longer made time for Letty, knowing full well that his attentiveness kept her sound.

One day in frustration, Letty tried to restrain Jim from attending a church meeting. Resentment flared within her as she suggested, "Suppose the Lord told you to stay home tonight?"

Jim countered with, "He wouldn't do that," and left the house. As he drove into town, God said to him, "Supposing she's right?", but Jim dismissed the thought.

Coming to the realization that their marriage was in trouble again, Jim and Letty went to a Marriage Encounter weekend. The seminar focused on communication tools and emphasized the principle that success is a journey and not a destination. The two shared some of their painful experiences with other couples in the class.

Letty found relief, knowing that others had similar difficulties. She wasn't so odd after all. The insight they received about who they were in the eyes of God brought a gentler understanding of themselves and each other. Letty started to see herself more clearly. She began to understand that she was a unique creation of God, and that she needn't strive on her own to overcome difficulties. Another realization hit her with sickening clarity: *All my idols have clay feet, my parents, my brother and my pastor, even Jim.* Cautiously, Letty began to relinquish control of her life and let God take the reins. She asked him to direct the path of her life and marriage. As God did this, the burdens and fears gradually became replaced with feelings of peace and purpose. Letty was on her way to recovery.

Jim began changing, too, and stopped trying to mold Letty into the person he thought she should be. Instead of being quick to judge, criticize, or get angry, he made a conscious effort to accept the ways in which Letty was different than himself. On the outside, this appeared to be a milestone. On the inside, Jim still harbored anger and resentment. Letty continued to need more attention than he was willing to give. When he saw he couldn't appease her with the best of efforts, Jim looked to God for answers.

His prayer became, "Lord, I will do, to the best of my ability, what you want me to do in our relationship. I won't do it for Letty, but I will do it for you." This time, he let God be in charge.

Healing for their marriage was not an instant miracle, but a work in progress. Years of painful memories and deep-seated suffering made for slow-healing wounds. Over the next few years, the journey continued. There were glorious peaks and some disappointing valleys. But, in concert, Jim and Letty found solid ground as their emotions steadied. "All in God's time," they reminded each other.

Today, their friends say there is a sense of peace and a sweet fragrance of Jesus in the Barnes' house. Love is no longer elusive. Jim and Letty read the Bible daily, pray, laugh, take walks, and travel together. Through God's grace, their intimacy and pleasure in one another has been restored.

In 2006, Jim and Letty celebrated their forty-fifth wedding anniversary and their relationship continues to flourish. There *is* a God who gets involved in the events of this world, and he has answered this couple's prayer.

Chapter 4
Number Games
The Story of Dan Hemmer

I knew it was *the* hand, the one I'd been hoping for from the second card dealt. We'd been playing Seven Card Stud all night long, and now I was not doing well. I was down about $500; it had been one of those nights. I started out great, but then the cards weren't mine. That was poker.

The sunlight was starting to peek through the blinds at Charlie's house in Nampa, and my eyes were pretty crunchy from about twelve hours of cigarette and cigar smoke. It was probably the last hand, but I knew I would win this one. With almost $800 on the table, it was left up to Dave and me.

I drew two aces down to start, and another was dealt up at the end, along with a queen, a jack, and a ten showing. My last card down was a five, but that didn't matter. I knew I had Dave beaten. He had nothing showing—a queen and a ten, an eight and a six, but I knew he didn't have anything else. Dave was the king of the bluff, but I knew I had him this time, and that $800 plus, was mine.

My heart was pumping wildly. "You gonna raise?" I couldn't help needling him.

"Call," he growled as he threw in fifty.

"Gotcha!" I thought, turning over my five and my two aces for a three of a kind. Dave looked resigned, turned his down cards over and my heart sank. He had a straight. It was over, I had lost.

Man that hurt, I thought, a little queasy as I figured out my losses— about $700. It was going to be a long ride home, into the sunrise, back to Boise. I wouldn't tell Barb, of course, but it always seemed easier to take the disappointment in her beautiful, blue eyes when I'd come home a winner after another all-nighter.

Although the exact memory of that night might be off a dollar or two, the point remains: I was addicted to gambling. Sometimes I won, sometimes I lost. The thrill of the challenge to win kept me thinking about gambling all the time. In fact, I lived for it. I even toyed with the idea of moving to Nevada to become a professional gambler.

It all started with numbers. You see, I'm good at numbers. I can remember phone numbers that I haven't called in years. I bet if people had numbers instead of names, I'd have no trouble at all getting those right. So it's logical that I'd get caught up in gambling, since it all has to do with numbers. I guess you could say it finally ended with numbers, too.

When I tell people about my addiction, they ask if it started when I was a kid, but it really didn't. Sure, my dad played poker and I bet on some billiard games when I was going to Boise State University, but I never really got into it until I was in the Navy. I was stationed at Fresno, California, and some of us were sent to Fallon, Nevada. That was the first time I had been to a casino.

It was almost sensory overload. Despite the haze of smoke, the glare of neon-colored lights was everywhere. Sounds of slot machines made the play seem alive, and somewhere in the background, there was the vague sound of a machine paying out. I looked around to see where the sound of coins dropping was coming from. A slot machine in the next aisle had a light flashing like a yellow emergency vehicle. An elderly woman was filling up a plastic container with her winnings, and I thought, *Wow, this is easy.* It was odd, but the players next to her barely even looked up.

So I tried some of the slots, and I won $300. That floored me. The Navy didn't pay all that well back in the 70's, and $300 was a lot of cash. I was hooked. Cashing out and stacking up my coin cups was pure fun. We didn't stay in Nevada for long, and later, I ended up on a ship off the coast of Vietnam for six months. There I didn't have a lot of chances to gamble, but back home in Boise, after the Navy, I remembered that thrill.

There's something about gambling. It is so exciting, it really gets your blood moving. It's all about more; the bigger the stakes, the higher the high. And it's never enough. You start out small, like betting a buck or two at the blackjack table, but the money has to get larger for you to get that shot of adrenaline. And so I remembered it all.

Soon after I married Barb, I pushed almost everything aside, and started living to gamble. I frequently drove to Tahoe and Vegas to gamble and play blackjack. Barb would go with me sometimes.

"Dealer bust. Player wins." It was easy to lose track of time when I was winning. I looked at my watch. I had been at the table for almost an hour. Some unconscious part of me realized it was time to go. *Oh, man, I was supposed to meet Barb for dinner tonight.* Showing unusual restraint, I walked away with my take.

Barb never gambled, and it was like we were on separate vacations when she came along. I got to the room and she was already dressed, waiting for me, watching TV.

"Hey, I'm sorry. I lost track of time." I really did feel bad. "I just won $300 at that last table, though," I said, hoping good news would soften her disappointment.

"Uh huh. Our dinner reservations are in twenty minutes," she answered. "Shall I call for a later time?" I could tell she was trying to hide her frustration.

"No, I'll be ready in ten," I promised, giving her a quick squeeze. I wasn't as anxious to keep the dinner reservations as I was to get dinner over with and return to the floor. I was confident even bigger winnings awaited me.

Eventually, I started to place bigger bets, especially on blackjack. I was getting good, after all, it's a game about remembering numbers.

I also started playing poker with my brother and some of his friends. He and his crowd always had a lot of money, at least more than I. I was working in construction and bringing home about $2,000 a month. He invited me to one of their poker games. I thought I could play really well, and they had lots of money for the winning. Later, I got involved in poker games at Charlie's house where the stakes were higher. I played most weekends, and it was wonderful when I won and terrible when I lost. Losing $400 to $500, or even more, in one night, when I was only making $2,000 a month, was hard. And it's sad because I never told my wife. I only told Barb about the times I'd win. "Hey, I won $500 last night!" But I would only say that I didn't do very well if I had lost. I hid the losses from her, too. I did the finances and the checkbook, and paid all the bills. Barb had little idea how much I would lose, and I won enough times that we never went broke. We always had enough to buy groceries. Although displeased with my gambling, Barb never said anything. She trusted me, so when I lost, I'd feel really guilty. I'm still ashamed because Barb deserved better than that.

I said that it was numbers that got me in and numbers that got me out, so I'll have to explain. In 1979, we sold our house to Kevin and Kim, a couple from California. Our lives sort of clicked, and we became friends. He and I would play racquetball, and I'd curse up a storm and throw a fit when I'd miss an easy point. I had quite the temper and a good supply of swear words.

Kevin, on the other hand, was a Christian, but he didn't push his beliefs on me. Instead, he used a mild humor to get his point across. Whenever I'd curse he'd say, "That'll cost you a point!" and we'd laugh about it.

One day, Kevin gave me a book, *Theomatics*, by Del Washburn and Jerry Lucas, formerly of the LA Lakers. It really interested me because it explained how numerically perfect the Bible was. They had discovered from the original Greek what the words meant numerically, and then somehow added them to get a perfect sequence. I started to think about the Bible as more than just any old book. You see, I never believed in God. Quite the opposite, I considered myself an atheist. I was always a loner kind of guy. I didn't need anybody to lean on. I could do it all myself. I just couldn't believe in all that God stuff. Who needed it? Not me! But somehow that book, and Kevin's example, started to work on me.

In December of that year, Barb and I went to Tahoe so I could play in a blackjack tournament. This was one of those two or three day tourneys that you were in until you lost, and I had won the first day.

"Let's get out for a while and walk," I suggested. It sounded good to Barb to get away from the casino. Fresh air would clear our heads.

"There's a bookstore. Let's check it out." Barb, a bookstore enthusiast, motioned to a sign a couple doors ahead of us.

"Sure," I shrugged. What could it hurt? She's been good enough to come on this trip, I could let her enjoy some book hunting.

It turned out to be a Christian bookstore, which was a first for me. I wouldn't have been caught dead in one back in Boise. I wandered among the shelves, but nothing caught my eye.

"Find anything?" I asked, hoping she was ready to go.

"This looks interesting," she said, picking up a book from the table marked Discounted Books. "It's only a dollar."

I turned the small book over in my hand, *How to be Born Again*, by Billy Graham. "Could be good," she commented. We were both curious about what it meant to be born again.

"Sure. Why not? Let's get it," I agreed.

With plenty of free time, Barb read it and so did I. The next day, I was back at the tables. In our hotel room that evening, Barb and I turned on the TV and there was Billy Graham again. Now I knew he was on TV all the time, but I never wanted to pay attention to him before. We listened for a while, and then he gave the invitation to receive Christ.

It was sort of strange. You hear about how emotional people get when they are born again, but for us it was more of an intellectual decision to do it. Why not, when it was so simple to do? The stadium was packed with thousands of people, and it looked like hundreds were getting out of their seats and walking down to the stage where Billy Graham was waiting to pray with them. So we got down on our knees in that casino hotel room and gave our lives to Jesus Christ. We just prayed what Billy Graham prayed, "Lord Jesus, I know I am a sinner and I need to be saved. I ask you right now to forgive me and I invite you into my heart as my Lord and Savior." It felt completely right.

The next day, I went back to the blackjack tables to try and win that tournament. I didn't feel much different, and it simply didn't occur to me, at that time, that my gambling was wrong. But I really wanted to win, so I had to bet a lot of money. In my last hand, I had $500 on the table—and I lost. The dealer had nineteen, and I had eighteen. But the strangest thing happened: she paid me anyway. She paid me $500! Although I didn't win the tournament, I walked away with $1,000. I thought about saying something, but the cards were already gone. I always felt that it was a sign from God, giving me a bonus for giving him my life.

I didn't stop playing poker for a while though. I was just too selfish to think about what Barb felt, or what it might do to my kids. It never even crossed my mind. But I stopped cursing right away. That was sort of a miracle. My anger and quick temper went away, too. That was a real blessing.

I finally did stop gambling. I kept thinking, *would Jesus want to be sitting next to me at these poker games that I can't afford?*

It was a good thing I quit, too. Barb later told me that if I had kept going the way I was going, she might have left me. She's been a very good wife to me. She put up with a lot and never harped on me about gambling. She just left it up to the Lord to help me, and I'm glad he did. A friend of mine gambled, and really got heavy with the betting. He lost everything. If it hadn't been for my new relationship with God, I could have lost everything also.

After years of not gambling, I began to play poker for dimes and quarters with my brother-in-law. This time it was for fun, and not the money. It was great fellowship, and I felt comfortable that gambling no longer had a hold on me.

However, I did make a mistake playing internet poker. I clicked on an icon that looked like a hand of cards over the words PartyPoker.com. A series of clubs, diamonds, spades, and hearts flashed on the screen until a message popped up: "Casino connected." It was so easy to get started, just a couple of bucks a bet, but soon enough, I started getting those old feelings back. It wasn't a lot of money, but I began to think about it all the time and looked forward to the times I could play again. The lights and sounds of the casino were missing, but the adrenaline rush of betting, and the potential to win even a few dollars started to capture me as much as the tables in Vegas had once before. Now, internet gambling is off-limits. It would be too easy to sit there and get hooked all over again.

Gambling can be a terrible addiction. It seduced me into caring about it more than anything else, even my marriage and my family. I'm thankful that Barb stayed with me all those years. I am forever grateful to my Lord,

60

Jesus Christ, for freeing me from that bondage. Jesus protected and covered me even before I believed in him. Fortunately, gambling never got to the point of ruining my life. It's humbling that he loved me enough to rescue me.

I get choked up thinking about an experience when I was in the Navy. I don't remember her name, but a woman at a shopping mall tried to give me a Bible pamphlet, and talk to me about Jesus. I blew her off. I didn't want anything to do with her, or God. She told me that I'd remember her some day, and I'd look back and see that what she said was the truth. I said, "Yeah, right," and walked away. But I still remember that meeting. If only her name were a number.

Chapter 5
Dancer
The Story of Geri Worthington

Bang! Clang! I winced at the sound of my new husband's inventive method of carrying our extra belongings. He strapped various household objects on the side of a rusty, old car he had found in a junkyard, and had attached an old washtub on the back. Somehow he got the old thing running, but what a sight we must have been. I felt like something right out of *The Grapes of Wrath*.

"Kinda noisy isn't it?" I asked, as I glanced at him sitting proudly behind the wheel.

"Well, what did you expect?" he snarled slightly. "I couldn't afford to buy a trailer and pay your way too. I don't know why you married me anyway." It felt like he had slapped me across my face. Stung and hurt, I slouched closer to the open window, hoping the hot breeze would dry the sweat on my dusty forehead. I probably smelled as bad as I felt. I decided against risking to ask if we could stop somewhere for a Coke.

I sighed and thought about his question. *Why did I marry him?* It certainly hadn't been love at first sight, like in my novels.

My first sight of Bernard, dragging his broken leg into the doctor's office where I was the receptionist, was not love. When he was injured, he somehow managed to drive himself for miles to get to the doctor's office. It wasn't all that odd really. In Homedale, Idaho, people were sturdy and self-sufficient, tough as the earth they farmed and accidents were

63

common.

Hoping my squeamish stomach wouldn't churn at the sight of his blood, I quickly wrote down his information and ushered him into an examining room. Bernard later told me that most of his subsequent visits for follow-up treatments had just been excuses to see me. But I had seen more than a man in physical pain that day. He seemed wounded somewhere inside and I felt sorry for him.

We dated for a few weeks after that, and he started pursuing me. I saw things that didn't seem quite right: he was compulsive, he blew up easily, and he wasn't apologetic about his behavior. As events unfolded, we ended up getting married, despite my misgivings. Now we were headed for our new home. To my utter amazement, that old heap of rust on wheels got us to Seattle.

"We'll be there soon," Bernard's voice broke into my reverie. "We'll be sharing kitchen and bath space with another couple, so make sure you help out."

"Of course," I replied obediently. I was determined to be a good wife.

We shared a dormitory directly across the street from the college with three other couples. Our first child, Gerald, was born during the two years we spent in this co-op style living arrangement.

Bernard took a full load of classes and worked full-time besides. Under this stress, his anger became physical. Often, I would find him asleep on the floor. Feeling sorry for him, I'd try to wake him to go to bed. But he'd slap angrily at me and growl, "I'm not asleep!" Sometimes he'd throw a few choice swear words my way. His reactive nature left me puzzled and confused. *If I could just learn the right way to approach him,* I thought, *he wouldn't get so angry at me.*

Bernard's rage shook my confidence. I doubted that I

Dancer

was a good wife, and sometimes I even doubted that I was a good person.

After he graduated, we headed for Indian Valley in northern Idaho. This time our cargo included the usual household belongings in a small trailer, plus two little boys: Gerald, the two-year-old, and Frank, just a year old.

Pulling up to the house where we were supposed to live, I felt a gasp escape my lips. "You must be joking!" I wailed before I could think to clamp my mouth shut. It hadn't taken long to learn the value of keeping my opinions to myself. But this! This broken-down, old house in the middle of nowhere had nothing around it but packed dirt and a few scraggly weeds poking up here and there. "Where are these little ones supposed to play? In the mud?" I asked, shuddering.

Perhaps Bernard felt the same way and my revulsion gave him a face-saving escape, for we left without ever unpacking. Back in Homedale, I suffered the blame for Bernard's failure to take a perfectly good job. "You aren't a good enough wife," others accused. "Be careful, you're thwarting God's plans!"

What does God have to do with this? I wondered. *Have I done something wrong? Surely I'm right to expect to have a decent place to raise our children!* But I was not really sure about anything. I was trying to survive. As my life slowly crumbled into bits and pieces, I longed for something better.

On the way to church one day, I dared to disagree with Bernard. Like a slingshot, his arm whipped across the seat, striking my face. Stunned, I assumed we would turn around and go home. But we drove on to church where I unsuccessfully tried to shroud what had happened. As other church members observed my anguish, Bernard went about his salutations and pleasantries. The pastor read right through my contrived smile and knew exactly what Bernard had done. *God, do you see me, too?* I wanted my husband's anger to stop, but I was too ashamed to ask anyone for help.

After this, the church leaders began conducting marriage classes in which the men were taught to love their wives, maybe even by (gasp!) helping them in the home. *Someone knows my plight,* my heart sang. I felt less alone. I was hopeful, because I knew others cared about me in my situation. *I just need to be patient and try harder,* I convinced myself. I was sure things would change, now that Bernard and I had some good teaching about marriage.

One day a friendly neighbor dropped by with a peck of cucumbers, which was customary when one found oneself with a bumper crop from the garden. Lacking a good recipe for putting up pickles, I decided to wait and get a recipe from a friend.

That night, Bernard trudged in the back door and spotted the cucumbers still in the same place. I saw the familiar look in his eyes that signified the slow burn that would crescendo into madness. He spied a piece of garden hose the boys had dragged in, and Gerald took his usual spot hiding under the bed. But this time would be different. As Bernard swung the hose over his head winding up to strike me, Frank, not yet three, ran toward his father and grabbed his arm.

"No! Daddy, no!" he wailed. The break in the routine slowed Bernard. Looking down, puzzled, he pushed Frank away and raised his arm again. But Frank was not to be stopped. Again and again, they did this dance until Bernard shoved me into the bedroom and slammed the door shut. A determination was born that day in the little boy's heart that never left. He shoved the door open, challenging his father.

Dancer

They went back and forth again and again until Bernard's anger started to dissipate. I was unaware of the far-reaching effects these events had on my children. *I'm taking the brunt of the abuse*, I thought. *I'm protecting them.* But Frank would tell me years later how this one incident was seared in his memory.

Not to be completely defeated, Bernard began the vicious tongue-lashing that was incomprehensible. He just needed to vent. Sometimes it would last for hours on end. He would make me stand still, not moving a muscle, as he berated me, but I had the ability to shut most of it out. My boys, however, wept with fear and helplessness as I waited to be "dismissed." Sometimes while I waited for the raving to wind down, I would pray. *God, do you care about my kids and me? What should I do?*

When things got really bad, I'd call the police for help. They did the best they could to calm Bernard down. Only once did he go to jail, but usually they just cautioned Bernard, and then left.

"I'm sorry," Bernard choked out an apology. He sat at the kitchen table after the police left. "I don't know what got into me," he said, shaking his head.

I wanted to believe him. Surely under all that anger there was a good man, a decent man. *What do I need to do to keep him calm?* For some reason, I felt it was all up to me to make him a better person. Very soon, this became a regular cycle. After a call to the police, we'd have a few months of calmer waters in the home. But when the storm returned, as it always did, it had grown in intensity.

One day, it was ten-year-old Frank who called the police. "Don't you EVER do that again!" his father screamed at him, terrifying him so badly that he never did.

The next time, we called my brother-in-law for

help. He tried to intervene and was rewarded with one of his teeth being knocked out. Somehow, I was unaware of the damage it was doing to the kids. Also, flickering moments of tenderness from my husband served to keep the spark of hope alive in my soul that things would eventually get better.

"I just want to have a nice life," Bernard mumbled. "You're so strong." But I didn't feel strong at all. "Things will change," he promised. *Why do I always believe him?* And yet he seemed contrite and sincere. I felt I should overlook his faults. He was the man. He was the one in control.

He couldn't control his own body though, and he developed seizures at night. He hid it from the railroad for a while, but it eventually was discovered. No longer able to work for the railroad, vocational rehab sent him to college where he excelled in his studies, earning a teaching degree.

"Where are you?" came the vicious voice I dreaded. Hiding under the kids' bed, I listened until his voice quieted. After a night's sleep, he'd calm down and I could come out. Sometimes I slept in the car. If I called the police, Bernard would lose this job. I was already daily taking the brunt of his anger, due to his inability to handle classroom discipline. *How had this happened to me? Had God forgotten me? Did he care?*

One night, I broke down sobbing in despair. Some friends sat quietly while I finally let out the fullness of my anguish. After continual berating from Bernard, I had no confidence left. I was trapped with no place of refuge, and no money. I had no options. Most of all, I was too weary to go on.

"I'm a failure," I sobbed. "I can't get Bernard to change. I can't keep the peace at home. I can't even protect my children."

Dancer

"It's time for you to get out of this situation," one friend gently advised.

My heart caught in my throat. "You mean I can do that? Will God help me?" *I got myself into this mess. How could I expect God to get me out of a situation I shouldn't have gotten myself into in the first place?*

"God loves you, Geri. He cares about you and your children." Hope soared within me. "When we ask God, he promises to make a way of escape for us."

"I had never considered asking God to get me OUT of this," I admitted.

I called my mother in California and tried to explain my decision. She was unsupportive. Undaunted, I ran to the beam of light that suddenly shone in my dark world. My younger brother sent fifty dollars to get me started on the way.

I took our three youngest—Debbie, Cecil and Cindy—to Nampa, Idaho. Frank was away at college. It was 1970 and the country was in turmoil over the war in Vietnam. Gerald, as the oldest, had gone and never returned. The chunk of my heart that had his name written on it was torn out.

When we were apart, Bernard seemed different. He said kind things to me. His attitude changed and he started trying to woo me back.

"I know now that I didn't let you and the kids live your own lives," he admitted sheepishly.

Whoosh! The air left my lungs and hope soared once more.

That summer, Bernard came to where I was living to retrieve his car. My mother was visiting and informed him I wasn't at home. She took the opportunity to set things straight. For the first time, she saw the look in Bernard's eyes

69

that I had tried to describe to her.

"I thought he was going to hit me!" she exclaimed to me later.

"You're lucky he didn't," I replied. She finally understood.

Bernard and I got back together, but his rages started up immediately. I reminded him of the sweet things he had so recently said to me about not letting us live our own lives.

"I never said anything like that," he bellowed. I knew then that it was a terrible mistake to think we could be together. Bernard continued yelling. Frank, home from college that day, raced up the stairs from the basement and saw his father about to strike me. He grabbed his father's hand.

"Don't hit her. Hit me!" He dared to challenge his father three times as Bernard raised his hand toward me.

Finally, Bernard turned on his son. Frightened that Frank didn't know what he was asking for, I ran to the phone to call the police. But the thrashing between father and son ended with Bernard on the floor and Frank on top of him.

"Stop, you're hurting me," Bernard begged. Years of frustration and anger were buried deep in Frank's soul and he wouldn't be denied. Frank held his father down for a long time, until he had made his point and his father had accepted it.

By now it wasn't considered as shameful to seek help, and someone suggested that a psychologist in Caldwell might be helpful. "Why did you want to go back to this man?" he wanted to know.

"Because we still have three children at home... It's hard to throw away twenty years of marriage... I thought he had changed..." My list went on and on. But I knew deep down that something in our relationship had to have once been whole for it to have a chance of being repaired. And it never was whole.

This time, I had all of my family's support and was able to move with my children to California, near my parents. Still, when Bernard and I divorced, I couldn't shake the feeling that I had let God down. That somehow, if I had worked harder, if I had prayed for Bernard more, if I... if I...

After a few years, I thought I could live a simpler lifestyle in Idaho than I had in California. I moved back, got a job with the State, and began attending a support group called Parents Without Partners. There I met Howard and we got married. Together we searched for a church, and a co-worker told me about one that met in a warehouse. We began attending Boise Valley Christian Communion. It felt like the place I had been looking for my whole life. God seemed real there, and people were genuine. I began to feel a peace in my life.

Then one Sunday, Bernard showed up at church.

Immediately, I stiffened. *What's he doing here?* I felt angry. *This is MY church! How dare he come here!* I felt he was encroaching upon my territory. Then I realized I had not been able to forgive him for those years of abuse.

I couldn't do it. When I tried to pray, I felt angry. That made me feel guilty. The old voices began to play in my head. My mother had controlled me through guilt. Bernard's family tried to use guilt to get me to stay in that abusive marriage. Ultimately, I wallowed in my own self-inflicted guilt. *If I had worked harder, if I had been more tolerant, if I... if I...*

"Some people have been so hurt in life," the speaker at church explained, opening his hands and spreading his fingers apart. "They begin to close like this." He curled his fingers into a tight fist. "You start hiding to protect yourself." I knew he was talking about me. "And when we close ourselves off to people, we close ourselves off to God's love also."

God loves me! This is real. God was not laying all this guilt on me. I was taking it on myself. The Bible says God is the one who blots out our wrongdoings, for his own sake, and remembers our sins no more. *Yes, God, I accept your forgiveness.*

After I accepted God's forgiveness, I had to forgive myself. Then, gradually, I forgave Bernard, but not because he deserved my forgiveness. I thought, *I can forgive Bernard because Jesus loves me and he's forgiven me.* Forgiving Bernard set me free.

In 1991, my second husband died, leaving an empty place in my heart. I was alone again. But this time, I was not afraid to ask for God's help. In the Bible, I read a verse that changed the way I look at God. "You have turned my mourning into joyful dancing. You have taken away my clothes of mourning and clothed me with joy." I think if Jesus were standing here in physical form, instead of just in my heart, he would probably be my dancing partner. I can hear him now. "Will you follow my lead?"

Chapter 6
The Pursuit
The Story of Denae and Morgan Kudera

I awoke with my skirt around my waist and a pounding headache. Rubbing my temples, I tried to clear away the cobwebs. I saw only the faces of strangers, a man and a woman. *Who are these people? Where am I?* I sprang out of bed quickly. Out of the corner of my eye, I noticed the man I had met last night at the bar, walking around the room. *I must get out of here immediately*, I thought.

Disjointedly, I stepped out from the dimly lit room into the bright sunshine. Squinting at the contrast, I began to gain my bearings. I trudged along the several miles of Mexican countryside, tears falling freely all the way back to my hotel room.

How did I end up here? I remembered drinking and laughing, then suddenly looking around and realizing my friends were gone. This guy who was buying me drinks offered to help me find my way back to my hotel room. The next thing I distinctly remembered was climbing over a white picket fence and thinking, at the time, that something was amiss, but I was too out of it to comprehend what might be wrong. The rest was a blur. Heck, my mushy mind was stretching its limits just trying to remember my name.

I decided I would simply never speak of this horrifying experience ever again. Putting it out of my mind would have to work, since I knew of no other way of dealing with the awful pain and humiliation. It's too bad things are never as simple as we wish.

"Denae, what are you thinking about?" asked Lisa, glancing at me quizzically.

"Oh, nothing," I said, shaking my head despondently, trying to get the offensive image out of my mind. It was our last night in Mexico, but I just couldn't bring myself to go out with the other girls. Nothing was worth celebrating after the ghastly experience of last night, but I could never tell them that. In fact, there were many things I wasn't able to face right now, things I wasn't even able to tell myself.

I had always been a good manipulator, able to make others believe whatever I wanted them to. As long as I didn't think anything was wrong, no one else would think there was either. *Why would it be any different now?* I wondered.

When I was in the midst of getting high, smoking pot, drinking, and doing mushrooms or acid, it was easy to pretend I was happy. I was on top of the world and, later, had the most wonderful memories. Unfortunately, that's all I had. To stay that happy, I had to get up and go do it all over again. It seemed there was no escape from the never-ending cycle; the pursuit of happiness became a full-time addiction. I tried to convince myself I was happy.

I had my first drink at age twelve and tried pot when I was thirteen. By fifteen, it had become routine and so had lying. Maintaining good grades and convincing my family and friends that I was still doing well became effortless over time. The more accustomed to drug use I became, the easier it was to hide. By the time I was eighteen I had a fake ID. My friends could only imagine the scene that was becoming familiar to me.

After high school, I moved into an apartment near campus with some college friends. I no longer went to church. We partied, free from the restraint of church, and I no longer had to hide my revelry from my parents. I didn't do

The Pursuit

well in college. High school had been a breeze, but Boise State University was much harder and I didn't have time for studying.

Most of the girls had parents who provided them with money, but I needed to find other means of funding my habits. Constant partying does have a price. Before long, I was in debt and dropped out of BSU. While my parents were on vacation, I moved back into their house. My life remained the same. Parties and deception fit me like an old familiar glove. My friends and I planned a trip to Mexico. As soon as I earned the money for my share of the trip, we were airborne, heading toward our dream vacation.

In Mexico, we could all drink legally, and we took full advantage of it. Every night there was a party going on somewhere. Clubs were hopping all the time and open until 4 a.m. It didn't matter that we had come to Mexico with no dates. There seemed to be an abundance of friendly guys who were eager to party with the *Americanas*. They bought us tequilas, which mingled well with the laughter of the nightlife.

With only two days left in Mexico, we headed out for another night of clubbing. Loud music permeated the open-air cantina. After several hours of dancing and drinking, I felt as if I needed to head back to our room. But when I looked for my friends, I found we had gotten separated. Unsure of the way back to my hotel, I followed the stranger who later raped me as I was passed out drunk, dead to the world.

I was in no mood to party our last night in Mexico. My humiliation over the previous night's events was too much to handle. I'd party again when I got home. For the moment, I needed some time to feel safe.

Within a few weeks, I knew there was no hiding

from this. I mentioned my concern to my closest friend. "Lisa, I think I might be pregnant."

"What? No way!" she countered immediately. She could not even fathom the possibility of my pregnancy. I had no boyfriend, and I certainly had not told any of my friends about what had happened in Mexico. Even though I persisted, she saw no reason for my anxiety.

"Look, I can't explain it. I just might be, that's all," I repeated.

Eventually, she tired of my paranoia. "Fine. Let's just buy a pregnancy test and find out for sure." Like the good friend she was, she waited with me for those three lengthy minutes it took to get the results.

"I can't look," I said. I felt as if I were glued to the couch. "You go check," I pleaded.

A moment later, Lisa came out of the bathroom, and the look on her face confirmed my deepest fears. *How am I to support and raise a baby at only twenty years old? I can't even take care of myself.* I had a heavy heart.

My first response was to get up bright and early the next morning, go to Birthright Crisis Pregnancy Center, and double check my results. Often, when I was inspired by alcohol, I had gotten on my soapbox, telling my friends why abortion was wrong. My Christian upbringing gave me a passion about it. Seeing a close friend overdose on drugs following an abortion further reinforced my conviction.

"It's positive. You're going to have a baby," the counselor said as happily as she could when she came back to where I waited. I was silent. I felt as if there wasn't enough air in the room. "I can see from your face that this was not a planned pregnancy," she continued. "We will help you in every way, if you need us." Though she offered me help in many ways, I didn't hear a word she said. I nodded and tried to thank her. I needed to get out of there. Back at home, I felt trapped. I didn't believe in abortion, but I wondered what other options I had.

"Do you think if a woman was raped, that God would understand if she had an abortion?" I tried to hide my problem by asking my sister a theoretical question.

Nicole turned to me with wide-eyed acceptance. "Oh, Denae, God *loves* your baby!" There was no way she could have known. But the truth hit me hard. I knew I could never abort this baby.

I had no idea how I would face my parents. The next day was my mom's birthday, and this wasn't the present I had intended to give her. I knew they suspected something was wrong; I wasn't keeping up my usual happy face.

Leaning against the doorframe, I took a deep breath. "Mom, Dad, I have something to tell you," I started. They looked at me, as if they already knew what I would say. "I'm pregnant."

I braced myself for the inevitable anger. This was by far the worst trouble I had ever been in. I couldn't believe their reaction. "We're here for you, Denae. We love you." Their acceptance broke down the wall of my self-protection. Immediately, the dam broke and I couldn't stop the tears. Although I expected disapproval, they offered me forgiveness and love as I poured out my story.

Alone in my bedroom that night, I tried to pray. I could not even imagine praying again. I contemplated in silence: *Where should I start? What would I say? Why would God even listen to someone like me?* I felt farther from God than ever before. My lips trembled with my inadequacy. I wanted to form words that might be appropriate for God's ears, but all I could say was, "God help me."

Quitting drugs wasn't hard, once I knew I was pregnant. I wanted to protect this baby from my abusive lifestyle, but losing my friends was much more painful. I grew closer to God, as my friends withdrew. I quickly realized how few friends I truly had, now that I was no longer choosing to party with them. In fact, except Lisa, all of my friends abandoned me. My heart ached for my lost friends, and I no longer had drugs to help me cope. It was an extremely difficult situation. They had been like my family, or so I had thought.

Reaching out for help, I started going to church with my family at Boise Valley Christian Communion, where I had grown up. The welcoming embrace people gave astonished me. How unworthy I felt when I walked back into the church for the first time in years. I was certain everyone's critical eyes would fall upon the pitiful blonde girl sitting in the third row. Yet I felt no judgment.

As time went on, I wanted to be upfront with people at church and tell my own story. The pastors were especially supportive, but when I approached them with my idea of talking to the congregation, they weren't too sure. They quickly voiced their concern. "Are you absolutely positive about this?" they inquired.

"Yes. I've prayed about it. I've talked to my parents about it, and I know this is the right thing to do." I was confident.

"There's no way to predict how people will take it. Most will understand, but a few might not," they cautioned.

"I realize that, but this is the church family that has stood by me when I completely rejected God. I want to start with a clean slate. I don't want people speculating about my situation or me."

The pastors relented and I prepared to tell my church the one thing I swore I would always keep to myself. Even though I had initially wanted to hide, I now passionately felt

The Pursuit

the need to live my life openly. The pastor said he would call me up when it was time. I waited, praying, in my seat. I tried not to think about what people's reactions might be.

Jolted back to attention, I heard the pastor talking. "Denae Pifari has asked if she could share with the congregation this morning, and we have agreed. Denae, do you want to come up now?"

Automatically I rose and waddled to the front, eight months pregnant, never taking my eyes off the cross at the back of the platform. I swallowed hard, determined to get the words out, as he handed me the microphone. Much to my surprise, the words flowed without reservation.

"Most of you know I haven't been living as a Christian these past few years. And I know many of you have prayed for me. Thank you. I'm here today to tell you my story and to ask your forgiveness." I explained my situation and breathed a sigh of relief. For a few seconds afterwards, there was silence. I felt as if I might be in the eye of a hurricane. Then Pastor Scott reached out to me in a hug and said the words I longed to hear.

"Denae, we forgive you."

What happened shocked me. Slowly at first, and one by one, loving faces from the sanctuary affirmed me. Someone spoke out, "I know the plans God has for you, plans of good and not of evil to give you a future and a hope." I couldn't believe it.

Then another from the far left side stood up and called out, "God is your strength and your fortress."

And then another stood, "May you and your baby be blessed. May God protect you and give you health." One by one, people stood all over the sanctuary and called out blessings over my baby and me. The outpouring of love from the church was unbelievable.

How different this was from my previous church experiences. Before, my mind would be a million miles away, thinking of buying a bag that night or the party I would be attending later, anything to distract me from the preaching going on just a few feet away. Now, I was fully involved in the moment, no longer tuning out God or the people around me.

At church, week after week, the music brought fresh tears to my eyes; all the songs seemed to speak directly to my heart. *Will I ever be able to make it through a service without crying?* I mused inwardly. Emotionally my life was a wreck, but God was rebuilding me.

After my baby, Morgan, was born, I decided to make a full commitment to Christ. *I've tried it my way long enough, now I will try God's way*, I thought. I simply prayed and surrendered.

"Jesus, I cannot rule my own life. I don't want to be in charge. Make me the person you want me to be. Make me a good mother for Morgan." I have always been very competitive, working to be the best, and this goal was no different. I was accepted into a missionary school, Youth With A Mission, which was going to Costa Rica. I began preparing for our trip and planned to take one-year-old Morgan with me.

During this time, I was still in emotional pain. I felt as if I were used goods, that no Christian man would want me for a wife. After much inner wrestling and prayer, I accepted the fact that I might never get married, that Morgan, the Lord and I could get by on our own. When I returned home a year later, I was confident about Morgan's and my future. I would get along just fine in life without a husband for me, or a father for Morgan.

Picking up my high school athleticism again, I joined a soccer team where I met Tom. Handsome, with lively, blue

The Pursuit

eyes and a ready smile, he was the team's soccer coach. As we sat and talked over lunch at Burger-N-Brew, I realized he was not controlling or threatening, which was quite a contrast from my former relationships. Tom was a good friend and it wasn't long until I began to think of him romantically.

I earnestly spoke about the great things God was doing in my life since I had turned it over to him. Many people were scared away by my talk of religion, but Tom was not one of them. He and I were able to talk about God and the impact he had made in our lives. It was nice to be able to bond that way with one another.

Our friendship evolved into a more serious relationship, and a year later we were engaged. Another year, and we were walking down the aisle. The Lord had brought Tom into my life as he had planned all along.

Tom was also adopted, so he has bonded with Morgan and can relate to her on that level. Tom, in turn, has now adopted Morgan and he is a wonderful father to her. It is especially meaningful for her, since she will never have an opportunity to know her biological father.

Morgan's story:

Coming home from the third grade one day, Tom and my mother were both sitting on the couch, and said they wanted to talk to me. Their grave expressions made me realize how serious this discussion would be. I was very concerned, wondering if I had done something wrong.

"Morgan, do you know who your biological father is?" my mother asked me.

"Yes, Tom is my dad," I said, telling her what I was sure she wanted to hear.

"Yes, but do you know that he is not your biological

father?" my mom asked, grasping my hands. She began telling me about some lady who had done bad things down in Mexico, and who was taken to an unfamiliar place by a man she had just met. The man who took her there ended up hurting her. The lady realized later on that she was going to have a baby. At the end of the story, they told me she named her baby Morgan. Before she finished the story, it clicked with me that Denae was the lady in Mexico.

I guess I had always known Tom wasn't my real dad, but I didn't think about it and had simply put the fact out of my mind. Until this conversation, I had been able to ignore it completely and not take any notice.

Between this conversation and the sight of my new blonde-haired, blue-eyed baby sister a few months later, I was strongly reminded of the fact that I was different from my family. They all had the same features, and then there was me with my curly, dark locks and beautiful, brown eyes. At least that's the way I had always viewed myself up to this point, but now I found myself starting to detest my dark looks. They seemed to send clear messages that I was different.

"Hey, Morgan, is that your new baby sister?" my classmate asked.

"Uh-huh. Her name is Kristan." Aware that everyone likes babies, I tried to be excited, too.

"Wow. She doesn't look anything like you. Where did she get those blue eyes?"

"From Tom," I responded, purposely saying *Tom* instead of *Dad*. I became really disconnected from my family and withdrew into deep depression and despair. My anger and resentment grew, especially toward Tom. When being disciplined by him, I screamed to myself, *you're not my father! What right do you have to speak to me that way?* I coped by shutting out the world, locking my anger and hatred within, until one day my mom saw me sulking in my room.

"Do you have any questions about anything?" she asked.

"Yes," I simply stated. The care in my mother's eyes stirred up my wrath and pain, she had no idea how I felt. I had learned to keep my anger in check, so I chained it down, but I kept talking.

"You know, everyone says how different I look from my siblings." Mother seemed to sense what was coming. "Since Kristan and Nathan have a different father, wouldn't they be my half brother and sister?" We both broke down and cried together for a full five minutes. With bunched-up Kleenex, we shared what we were feeling. For me, the anger lingered.

About a month later, feeling cold and alone, I stood shaking in my room, crying out to the Lord in Latin, a dead language, but still fitting. "Ubi es Deus? Ubi es?" which means, "Where are you, God? Where are you?"

"I am in all places and I am with you." The words seemed to echo around the room. The voice had the strength of a mountain and yet was as soft as a butterfly sneeze. Surprised, I sat rigid for a moment before feeling the smallest glimpse of heaven. I felt complete. God pushed away all my concerns and, for a second, no time existed.

It's still hard for me to deal with the fact that I will never know my biological father, but God has helped me. I have forgiven my biological father. God erased my fears and he is there for me even when I don't feel it.

My mom said people brought Bible verses along with their presents to my baby shower. She saved those verses for me in my baby book. One scripture, in particular, kept reappearing: I know what I'm doing. I have it all planned out,

plans to take care of you, not abandon you, plans to give you the future you hope for. When you call on me, when you come and pray to me, I'll listen. When you come looking for me, you'll find me. Yes, when you get serious about finding me and want it more than anything else, I'll make sure you won't be disappointed. I'll turn things around for you. I'll bring you back from all the countries into which I drove you, bring you home to the place from which I sent you off into exile. You can count on it.
Jeremiah 29:11-14

Chapter 7
Stepping Back
The Story of Dave Hobson

Windows down, radio blasting, this was a great moment in a string of great moments. My best friend, Yukon Jack Canadian whiskey, was by my side on the road between Meridian and Boise. As we neared home, I knew an empty bottle couldn't arrive with me. Checking the rearview mirror and then the side mirrors, I made certain no other cars were nearby. Then I hurled the incriminating container out the window.

This deception was my daily ritual as I drove home each day. I was blind to the empty bottles and broken glass with which I littered the roadside and marked my customary route. The sparkling trail to our driveway was the metaphor of a life marred by addiction. Steeped in alcoholic deception, I thought I was in control and undetected. But this free-falling deception eventually led me to lock myself in the bathroom with a shotgun. Even that was not the bottom.

While my dad served in World War II, my mom moved us from Seattle to her parents' home in Payette, Idaho. Living with her parents provided comfort, and unconfined, wholesome outdoor play in rural Idaho. With loving parents, close family, and a boy's dream environment, I had a great childhood by any measure.

My brother and best friend, Bob, and I designed our own entertainment. We were often left to our imaginations, which was generally positive. The one serious licking I ever received came after our reunited family was living in Boise. Bob and I stole a nudist magazine from the Rexall Drugstore. We hid in a field behind a nearby office and played with matches, setting fire to selected anatomical parts pictured. Then the field caught fire! Good, red-blooded American boys were saved from themselves by the fire department's quick response. The price of this tomfoolery was an equally quick, robust strapping from my dad's leather belt.

That was hard love, but most of the love in our household was a softer, slightly diffused pastel memory. Mom and Dad were there for me, helping with homework, Boy Scouts, baseball, and reading stories at bedtime.

"Jesus loves me, this I know, for the Bible tells me so." I clearly recalled this from Sunday school. I was introduced to God through family worship in church. Grandfather was a Methodist minister. I participated in Sunday school, children's choir, and Methodist Youth Fellowship. My parents were stable, God-fearing people and not alcoholics, contrary to the typical background for Alcoholics Anonymous participants. Deception crept into my habits as I grew up, negating a wonderful childhood brimming with promise and parental guidance. I had been introduced to God, but I did not follow him.

Deception led to my first marriage. My idol was not Jesus, but James Dean. I spent my lunch hour hanging out across the street from Boise High School, trying to look cool. I sported a ducktail, rolled my cigarettes in my shirtsleeve, and wore my jeans low. At fifteen, I managed to attract a cute cheerleader. We were soon in love. I often lied to my parents about where I was going, and then drove into the lonely, dark foothills with my girl-

Stepping Back

friend. A tire went flat on one outing, so I thumped-thumped on the flat all the way down to Harrison Boulevard. From there, I called my folks with a concocted explanation of accidentally bashing a curb.

Eventually, at sixteen years of age, I learned I was to be a father. Marrying was the honorable option in 1960. Abortion was not openly considered. We wedded secretly before a Justice of the Peace in Boise. No friends or relatives were present at the antiseptic ceremony. No honeymoon afterwards, either. We embarked on married life by separately retreating to lonely beds at our individual family homes. I confessed only after my wife's pregnancy became obvious. I dropped the bomb at the dinner table.

"Mom, Dad. My girlfriend is pregnant, but don't worry, we're married."

Dad and Mom poured guilt on themselves for their son's choices. We got married again in our family church.

With adult life thrust upon us, I enlisted in the Air Force, leaving my wife and daughter in Boise. In the service, I began drinking, beginning with beer, the lubricant of barracks life. It was ever-present and always used.

Government pay brought with it the ability to live off base with my family, but the drinking continued. One drunken Saturday, I threatened my neighbor over something insignificant—water run-off. In retaliation, he jumped in his car trying to flatten me.

In a panic, my wife called the police. "My husband has a knife!" The officer saw little humor in the dust-up.

"We're taking him to jail, Ma'am." They explained, "You can come down and post bail later."

87

"Keep him in there. Let him cool down," she retorted unsympathetically. We separated shortly after this event. I moved on base to slosh through an alcoholic life of barracks parties, and drunken sprees in border towns. Often, I was unable to find my car the next morning after awakening in strange places.

My wife and I reconciled while I was stationed in Tampa. Our love blossomed again in a period of relative sobriety. I developed a habit of drinking for a period, then quitting, only to resume the cycle later. We sought out a church and I remained dry for two years. As I learned later, one of the first steps in redemption from addiction is to turn control of your life over to a higher power who, for me, was God. *That's okay for my family*, I mused, *but not for me!* I was not letting a higher power control me. I was controlling me, or so I thought. Ultimately, predictably, I failed. In drunken stupors, I would walk the neighborhood. Once, stopped by police as a possible suspect in some nearby vandalism, I was jailed for the night. Under these circumstances, our marriage ended in 1973. I knew divorce wasn't right; it did not fit with my spiritual upbringing. Even at this juncture, I refused to listen to that inner voice saying, "Acknowledge who you are and what you are. The truth will set you free."

I maintained an intellectual relationship with God. My early upbringing influenced my life, yet through this point in time, I had never felt God's love or a kindred bond. He was just there, like paint on the walls. No vestige of religion was apparent in my life. Four years later, I met and married Bobbie. Over the next few years, she embraced God after viewing a movie about Christ Jesus. Thankfully, due to her relationship with Jesus, she became involved in worship at Cole Community Church. I

Stepping Back

joined her there and even played violin with the church orchestra. Occasionally, I ducked rehearsals. Other times, I reeked of booze breath when I did show up. More and more my life revolved around alcohol. I put it before everything else, including my wife. Yet, the lady I married had enough faith, grace and love to stand by me. She also sought support in the twelve-step program of Al-Anon.

For my part, I was impeccably selfish, alcohol my steadfast focus. In my couch potato persona, I drank myself into oblivion each night. I told my wife that I loved her, but this rang hollow in the long trail of deception and denial. Yukon Jack and Johnny Walker prevailed in any test of affection. Beer was history, replaced by hard booze after my first marriage. Secretly, I was frightened by how it owned me, and how I had given myself over to its power. I persisted in drinking even more heavily, until one sodden Saturday my wife feared that I was suicidal. I had grabbed my shotgun and retreated to the bathroom. She begged through the locked door, "Honey, come out. I love you. I called your brother. He's coming over."

Additionally, she called the Garden City Police who induced me to come out, saying, "Sir, if you don't come out of there we'll have to break the door down. None of us wants that." They confiscated the shotgun, much to the relief of my wife and terrified brother, who drove me to his house to sober up. Though, at my insistence, we went by way of the liquor store!

I knew I needed help as a drowning man, but it took one particularly humiliating event to initiate the desire for recovery. My wife arranged an intervention. Relatives and friends who knew of my addiction, but loved me enough to confront me, gathered in secret at my parents' home. Of course, I was totally surprised—

shocked—when I unsuspectingly stepped through the door. Everyone in the room knew my condition.

My stepdaughter spoke up, "Dave, you're a super grandfather to Zach, but it's getting so I'm afraid to leave him alone with you." That hurt, I loved my grandson.

My friend, Ken, added, "Buddy, I always know the days when you've been drinking when we step out onto the tennis court." I didn't think it was that obvious.

"When I tell you something, I have the feeling you're only half hearing me," another friend remarked.

I consented to begin my journey to sobriety by entering the addiction treatment program at St. Alphonsus Addiction Recovery Center. Deep within me, I harbored feelings of betrayal toward my wife for arranging the intervention. Rationally, I understood that she had not betrayed me, since my problem was obvious to everyone in my life. Thoughts of betrayal and blame shifting brought no balm. I attended that program, but a bottle was always close by when classes ended. Since I made no real decision to change my life, no change occurred.

A few years prior to retirement, I maintained an appearance of seeking sobriety through Alcoholics Anonymous meetings and participation in their twelve-step program. Nothing more than dancing with the devil came of this, since I did not maintain sobriety for any length of time. Drink, stop, drink, stop, and finally not stopping. I was immersed: bottom untouchable, shore nowhere in sight, and fantasizing about controlling my addiction after decades of saturation and abuse.

In drier moments, I rationalized and blamed outside influences for my addiction: the stress of work, pressure, ad nauseam. By the 1990's, I could retire when age and years in service as a teacher summed to ninety. My number was close, and I convinced myself and my wife that I could control the drinking; all would be well with the world if I just retired. Foregoing full benefits, I retired early, vainly refusing, once again, to admit the true reason for feeling beset by circumstances. I became afraid, and finally recognized my helplessness.

As my predicament crashed in upon me, I had nowhere to turn but to some other power or person. I begged my wife for help. I begged God for help. I understood self-control was beyond my grasp, that I could not manage the drinking.

I hit the final bottom during a two-day binge. Alone at home, I was drunk at 9 a.m. while my wife went to exercise class. When she came home, I cried, "Please check me in to Intermountain Hospital. I can't do this any more." I broke through the denial and reached for help.

It was not that I was *in* Intermountain Hospital, but that I was *seen* there by an acquaintance who did not know of my addiction. How awkward, how *embarrassing*. The public admission of helplessness, being discovered in treatment, was awful.

With this public admission, I understood the parallel admission that I must make to God for all the wrongdoings, and to all the people I had hurt. I had inflicted many wounds because my life centered on alcohol abuse. What I learned long ago, "Jesus loves me," surely was true. He had stood patiently by me, yearning for me to come to him. At last I could cry out to God, "Please, Lord, I don't know where to turn. But I know if I ask you to come into my heart and live there, you will come." And he did. What a blessing to know that he had stayed by me in his grace and mercy to the point when I yielded to

91

him. I was also blessed with Alcoholics Anonymous. I believe this is a God-inspired, spiritual program. The first three steps to recovery said, that after our lives became unmanageable, we stepped back and let God take over. What a relief to know I didn't have to be in control anymore.

God will not let go of me, but I must cleave to him. Every day I reach for his word, not the bottle. It's a choice I make daily. The once empty place filled by alcohol is now filled with Christ's love, instruction and wisdom from the Bible. Prayer keeps me in touch. My wife and I worship him and study his word together. I need this nourishment, for I know that to abandon God now would only open the door to my old weaknesses. In surrender to Jesus Christ, I now have life and freedom.

Chapter 8
Finding Home
The Story of Dan Clements

Life doesn't hold many options for a convicted murderer recently released from prison. Guards handed my stepfather his parole papers, his personal effects, and just enough money to rent a tiny, rundown apartment in the slums of Yakima, Washington.

Boarded up businesses and dingy shoebox hotels formed a backdrop for a community of outcasts. Hustlers and dealers lounged outside the pool halls and bars. Streetwalkers paraded up and down the cracked sidewalks. Ignoring the gawking high school boys, the hookers hoped to catch the eye of, and party with, the nervous-looking suits slowly driving by.

In this gray underworld my stepfather lived, and here is where I found my next fix of heroin. As I pushed the needle into my bulging vein, liquid warmth rushed to my head.

The milky haze quieted my tense nerves. My stepdad, the ex-con, gazed into my face and wisely asked, "What are you doing to your life, Dan?" The question shook me from my stupor. I had no direction, no hope.

Considering my background, it's not surprising that I ended up in this drug-induced fog. I was born to alcoholic parents, and Mom barely kept us fed as she went through drugs and five husbands. Life had no ground rules. My grandparents and extended relatives had died from drug and alcohol abuse. This was my family, the lost souls that made up my heritage.

In this setting, life's lessons began early.

"Get in here!" my mom hollered again. I refused to leave my lookout point on the front steps. "You're wasting your time."

"No! I know he's coming." I readjusted my seat on top of my suitcase. As the sky darkened to night, I had to admit that my dad wasn't coming. I knew he cared for me, but HE HAD PROMISED me. I believed him, but he hadn't come. The disappointment was sharp. I learned as a five-year-old boy that it hurts to be betrayed and that life isn't always what you want it to be.

I grew up rebellious, resenting and distrusting authority. By the time I was in seventh grade, I started smoking pot; add that to the booze that was always available at home, and I dropped out of school in the ninth grade. By eighteen, I was married with a baby on the way.

"Where are we going to go?" my young bride, Sandy, asked. She was understandably anxious. There was no work in the middle of winter in Yakima. Picking fruit was the only work I knew, and it wasn't an option that time of year.

"Don't worry. I've got a plan." I knew of one sure place that would offer me a job. The recruiter was more than happy to see me. The army would take anyone eighteen or older, with or without a high school diploma. While stationed at Fort Lewis, Washington, I settled down a bit. But the army never really straightened out my life like you usually hear about. I got paid every two weeks in cash, and that handful of twenty-dollar bills bought all the drinks and marijuana I wanted. Eighteen-year-olds could drink on base and drugs were plentiful. It was two years after the Vietnam War, and for some of the troops, morale was pretty low.

Finding Home

My drinking affected my service. Twice I made corporal, and twice I got busted back down because of alcohol. I couldn't maintain much of a home life. Sandy and I broke up within a couple of years. Finally I went AWOL, intending to return within thirty days, but never making it back. After thirty days, you were considered a deserter.

The Army will always find you. I knew I needed to deal with this. On my way to turn myself in, I stopped to see Sandy and our little girl, April. Sandy's dad knew I was AWOL and called the police. That's how I ended up spending ten days in the stockade.

Soon afterwards, on my twenty-first birthday, I met Kathy, who was just sixteen. After settling up with the Army, I began working in the construction field as a roofer. Kathy and I married, but neither of us knew how our love and commitment would be put to the test. We tried to work around the rough edges, as we were both from dysfunctional homes. By our eighth year of marriage, our house was busy with three children: one daughter and two sons.

"We can't keep going on like this, Dan." Kathy brought up the subject of my drinking and doping one more time. As always, I pushed Kathy away, not letting her get close to my empty heart.

"Leave me be! You've got a roof over your head, don't you? The kids are fed, aren't they?" I was a good provider for my family, always remembering the harsh times I had endured growing up.

"It takes more than a house and food to make a family. You spend more time at the bar than with the kids or me. I'm trying to make a life here!"

"Can't you just lay off me for a while?" I slammed the door and headed for the familiar safety of the bar. Unfortunately, I had the money to spend at the local bars and on whatever drugs I wanted.

Kathy knew I wasn't any good for the kids or for her either. My lifestyle robbed Kathy of friendships. If she got close to any girlfriends, I'd just end up having an affair with them. We separated and I was left to my own devices. Kathy went to live with her grandmother in Vancouver, Washington. Over the next few years, she and the children were in and out of my life, always hoping that I would change.

Drinking and drugs ruled my life during the times we were together in Yakima. *Just to get me going*, I'd think as I downed a shot of whiskey before work. Roofing is a rough business with rough men. We drank at lunch and we always headed to the bar after work. We were tough men who didn't have time for non-drinkers.

Eventually, I was laid up pretty bad in an accident. After falling off a roof at work, I had to go on Worker's Comp. I had injured my knee several times and after surgery, the doctor prescribed pain medication. It didn't take long for me to get addicted to the pain meds. I could not get drunk or high enough to forget the person I was turning into.

My stepmother, Shirley, was one person who really cared about me. She came to me one day and said, "Dan, why don't you and the family come with me on Sunday?" It was Easter and she attended the Foursquare Church. "I'm not saying you have to do anything there. Just come with me. You might like it." Shirley wasn't pushy, and I guess she got me at a weak point. Usually my heart was too hard to even consider such a thing, but I was curious.

"Sure," I shrugged. I had never been inside a church before. We went as a family to church that Easter. I figured I was probably the last person church people would expect to come through the doors, but I went. Despite being strung out on pain meds, the pastor's words from the Bible got through to me. When he offered people a chance to come forward and accept Christ as their Savior, I found myself walking down the aisle. I prayed with the pastor, "Jesus, I know I've messed everything up. I'm a sinner. Forgive me. I need you to save me." No angels sang that I could hear and no light came down from heaven. But when I walked back up that aisle to my seat, I knew something had happened. God had laid his hand on my life and honored my prayer.

Toward the end of the service, Kathy had stepped outside because the baby was fussy. As she listened to the service through the open doors, she heard a shout so loud she felt it reverberate: "Hallelujah!" She thought it came from the people in the church, but we never shouted. It was probably a shout from heaven over the fact that a sinner like me had accepted Christ. It was my first glimpse into a spiritual dimension.

Later, I tossed the last prescription of painkillers into a box and forgot about it. Yet my journey was not over. I was not ready to break away from the demons that held me. *I can't get into God*, I told myself, *because I won't be able to go out and get drunk*.

Within one month, I took a turn that distanced me even further from God. I started doing heroin and hanging around people who did it. Heroin grabbed me from the start. The rush was addicting, all my inhibitions crumbled, and I was ready to do whatever it took to repeat the experience.

Kathy realized that I was crawling into a dark hole that she couldn't rescue me from. She knew heroin was bad news. Her concern was for the kids, and she wanted me clean.

"Baby, I'm going to quit." I made the same promise over and over, only to break it again and again. This lifestyle was dangerous not only for me, but for my family.

One afternoon, the phone rang as Kathy was starting to make dinner. When she answered it, someone on the other end of the line identified herself as a caseworker. "Kathy, there's a bad situation brewing. You need to know your life is in danger. You need to get out of town."

"You mean pack up and leave? Just like that? How am I supposed to do that? I don't have any money and I've got three kids to watch out for."

"We realize that. That's why we are cutting you a check for $500. When you get the money, buy bus tickets and leave immediately."

Kathy agreed and hung up, wondering where she would go. She figured by the time she got the check in the mail, she would have a plan. A half hour later, the doorbell rang. A man from the caseworker's office identified himself as he handed her a piece of paper. "Here's your check," he announced as he turned to leave.

This is serious, she thought, *if they are bringing the money in person instead of mailing it.* She sprang into action, packed up the family once again, and left for Boise, Idaho.

I came home that evening to find dinner burning on the back of the stove and an empty house. On my own, with a new habit, I started selling everything in the house. I was hungry for this false sense of peace that kept me from facing my fears. Out went our furniture, even my children's toys. Nothing was left untouched. I sold it all to pay for my habit.

It was then, as I was shooting up at my stepfather's one-room apartment in Yakima, that he confronted me with that simple question: "What are you doing to your life, Dan?" Despite the heroin stupor, I remember his words as clear as a bell. "What are you doing? You have a wonderful wife and three lovely children."

Finding Home

My stepfather's words haunted me for days. I decided to ask God for help. "God, I'm going to call Kathy one more time and ask her if she'll take me back. But if I go home, I can't be like this anymore." It took me awhile to get up the courage.

"Hi, Kathy, it's me." I kept my voice steady.

"Dan, you're about the last person I'd expect to hear from." She paused, then added, "How are you?"

"About the same. I've been thinking about calling you for the last few days. I've got to ask you something." I felt her resistance on the other end of the line. "I want to get back together."

"We've been around this more ways than I care to number, Dan. You're crazy. You think you want to be with the kids and me, but really it's just that you don't have anywhere else to go. I'm through with it."

"But I'm away from the bad stuff now. It's not going to be like before." I wasn't stupid enough to think she would take my word for it. We argued a long time.

"I can't handle your craziness. I'm through with you cheating on me, running out on us, and hurting the kids like that." Everything she said was true.

"You're the one I want to be with. It'll be different. You'll see."

"You're so full of it. I know the minute you get here you'll be..."

I broke in before she could go on. "We'll be a family. Just give me a chance. You'll see." I was ready to promise her the moon if I had to.

"Okay, but I won't have drugs around the kids. Either you come home clean or don't come at all." Kathy's tone told me she meant it.

"I know. I know. I'm going to make all that up to you.

You won't be sorry." I was ready for change.

I sold everything except for my car and several boxes of personal items. A Bible that my stepmother had given me was still in its original cardboard package, unread. I grabbed my few possessions and piled them into the car. Then I added one last fix of heroin. *This'll be the last one*, I told myself before I jumped in the car.

Driving gave me time to think. I had let my family down. As the miles passed, my eyes kept darting to the heroin-filled needle carefully balanced beside me on the seat. *Was it possible to get free of my habit?* Stuck inside the car, I had about six hours to consider my future.

Cruising out of Baker, Oregon, on I-84, I again glanced at the heroin next to me. I kept saying, "God, you've got to help me. If I keep doing this, I'm going to be dead." Mile after mile I cried out to God, until my plea blended into the sounds of the pavement beneath me. "Help me. Help me. HELP ME." And he did.

Suddenly, I heard a very clear voice say, "Throw it away."

Before I had time to think, I rolled down my window, grabbed the needle, and chucked it out as hard as I could. An incredible feeling of relief swept over me as the needle flew from my hand. A warm chill up my back made me shiver, and I knew God was with me. My car was filled with an overwhelming sense of love. For the first time, I had a REAL encounter with God. All I could do was thank him, blinking back a tear.

I was almost to Boise and not sure of my welcome, but I was determined to fight my way to sanity as I pulled into the driveway. Kathy watched over me as I went through withdrawal. She warned the kids that I would be sick. Getting off heroin is an ugly process.

Finding Home

Needing to relax my tortured body, I remembered the prescription for my knee injury that I had saved. I found the unopened bottle of Darvocet that I had thrown into an old cigar box. There was enough for just four days, but I was thankful. It was enough to get me to the next level. I had no control over my body as it knotted and convulsed. At one point, Kathy chased me into the closet. In the dark, I hid while I battled the pain and the shame that I felt.

After coming clean, I was ready to get serious about God, but I wasn't sure how.

God heard my simple request for help and sent Dave to work with me, buying and selling antique furniture. We worked together with the antique business and hung out after work. Dave wasn't like other friends I had had in the past. He always seemed at peace, and I knew he wasn't getting it from a bottle anymore. That made an impression on me. *It must be God*, I reasoned. I wanted the level of spiritual strength that he had.

We talked about the Bible, God, and the Christian life. Dave had a way of talking that drew people's attention. If we stopped for lunch, Dave would pray in the restaurant. And he didn't pray some puny little quiet prayer. When he prayed he didn't care who heard him.

At times, sadness swept over me when I thought about the times Kathy had tried to talk to me about God. She had known God since she was a little girl. But when she brought the subject up, I'd walk away and tell her to stop because I didn't want to hear about God. Now I did.

After I started being real with God, I took up reading the Bible and the words seemed to jump right off the page. Jesus was just WAITING for me to reach out for his love. He didn't reject me or let me down. Still, there was no one I'd hurt more in life than Kathy, so she was skeptical at first. I didn't try to prove anything to her. Eventually, she believed I had given Jesus control of my life because she saw the changes. My focus had changed. In the old days it was me first, booze second, and maybe Kathy came third. Now it's God first, then my wife and my children.

My friend, Dave, was so happy to have my family and me in church with him. Eventually, he died of a brain tumor, the pastor retired, and Kathy and I began looking for a church of our own. One early November Sunday, we walked into Boise Valley Christian Communion and sat in the second-to-last pew. The woman sitting behind us prayed for us during the whole service. As soon as the service ended, she was right there in front of us.

"You need prayer," she declared matter-of-factly. We agreed.

This is what it feels like to have friends, I thought. We knew we were home.

Chapter 9
Perfect Timing
The Story of Diana Nelson

"I'm pregnant!" Julie squealed, amid hugs from women gathered in the entryway. "We're due the end of November," she gushed, answering everyone's next question.

"Is it a boy or. . ." the happy conversation went on without me. Unconsciously, I turned away before anyone saw my tears threatening to spill over. *Will I ever be the one telling the good news?*

God, do you hear me? I wondered, even as I answered my own question. *Of course he does.* But three years or thirty-six months or one thousand ninety-five days seemed like forever. Every day I saw mothers and children laughing together, and I turned to the sound of every baby's cry. Not a day passed that my mind didn't go there, my heart didn't ache, and my arms didn't feel empty.

Even as a child, being a mom seemed like the best thing in the world to me. When Lisa, my little sister, arrived, I was convinced she joined our family just for me. I mothered her, changed her diapers, and sang to her. I knew someday I would have my own houseful of active children.

My love of children drew me to pursue a career in speech-language pathology. I had an opportunity to work in schools in western Idaho, and attended Christian Life Fellowship in Ontario, Oregon. "Who's the guy over there in the blue shirt?" I asked, nodding toward the front.

"That's Scott Nelson, our youth pastor," my friend smiled at me. "Want to meet him?"

the ticket life-changing journeys

"Yes," I answered, trying not to sound too eager. It turned out Scott was interested in me also, and we began dating. We married six months later, just after I turned twenty-six.

My plan was to have children by age thirty, so we had plenty of time. Three years later, Scott took a pastoral position in Nyssa, Oregon, and we felt settled. *Now is the time to start our family*, I reasoned. I expected it would be no problem, since my mother's and sisters' children had arrived with no apparent difficulty. *Scott and I will be a family of three before my next birthday*, I happily concluded. I was adamant about one thing, though, and spoke honestly with God about it: "Father, give me only children who will walk with you. I could not handle any of my children going to hell."

Time passed. "It's been six months, Scott, do you think there is a problem?" I queried, not really worried, but wanting to know.

"These things can take time," he reassured me.

Another six months passed. "Lord, a year has gone by. I really want to be a mother by the time I am thirty." *That is a year away, so surely I will become pregnant before then*, I encouraged myself. It seemed as if everyone in our lives was falling in love, marrying, and immediately getting pregnant. I was happy for them, but my own wait seemed emptier.

Scott and I told only a few people about our frustration in getting pregnant. At the time, a friend of mine who was pregnant with her third child lost her baby. Her husband decided he didn't want another baby after the miscarriage, though she still longed for one. I told her my desire to have children and that we had been trying for some time.

"Diana, I know how much you and Scott want a

baby," she offered. Then she turned to me again. "At least *God* is saying no to you—not your husband!"

I jolted back. *Is God saying no to us?* I knew it was her pain speaking, but I wondered, *am I never to be a mom?*

In July, a young man shared a scripture he felt was meant to encourage someone in our group. I quickly grabbed my Bible and turned to Psalm 22:1-5, knowing it was for me. My God, my God! Why have you forsaken me? Why do you remain so distant? Why do you ignore my cries for help? Every day I call to you, my God, but you do not answer. Every night you hear my voice, but I find no relief. Yet you are holy. . . Our ancestors trusted in you, and you rescued them. You heard their cries for help and saved them. They put their trust in you and were never disappointed.

Tears of relief fell on my open Bible, as I turned my face upward: "Oh, God, you do understand my pain. Thank you, thank you." Suddenly, the world seemed brighter.

Shortly after that, I approached Scott. "What do you think about pursuing adoption? Do you think that is what God wants for us?"

He looked down into my questioning face. "Well, maybe it *is* time for us to consider other options. What about checking out medical counsel first?"

After the consultation, our doctor sat us down. "There doesn't seem to be a medical reason for you not to have children. If you don't get pregnant in another year, perhaps we might consider an in vitro procedure." *Another year!* Our eyes met with the same look of disbelief.

Scott and I knew complex medical procedures were not for us; we agreed to look into adoption.

At our request, an adoption specialist, Ed, from the

state of Oregon visited us. "Our department gets only four or five healthy newborns a year. Most newborns available for adoption are usually drug-addicted babies or have fetal alcohol syndrome." *No*, I thought, *that cannot be for us.* We agreed that we wanted our first baby to be healthy. Later we might consider adopting a special-needs child, but not as our first. *Maybe if we can find a baby through private means, we can find a healthy one,* I consoled myself.

That November we attended a conference in California. The speaker, John Wimber, told the group, "There is a couple here who wants a baby and will return next year with one." My heart skipped a beat. "That couple needs to come up front," he continued. Scott was grinning from ear to ear. Along with several other couples, we went forward. For the first time in a very long time, I felt hopeful.

Meanwhile, intent on the challenges in his job, Scott was not experiencing the same degree of agony about our childlessness as I was. That January, he decided to resign as pastor, and our lives were thrown into turmoil.

During this unsettled time, we heard of a private adoption possibility. My family attended Boise Valley Christian Communion, where a pregnant teenager in the congregation wanted to release her child for adoption. About the same time, we enrolled in a fifteen-session class required by the State of Oregon for pre-adoptive parents. During break time of our last session in February, the adoption specialist approached us.

"We just got word of a nineteen-year-old girl who is due to deliver a baby anytime," Ed said. We barely dared to breathe waiting for his next sentence. "Would you two be interested?"

"We have another possibility for a private adoption. We'll get back to you." Praying about the two potential adoptions, we felt confident God had a specific plan for each of these babies. He would direct us to the child meant for us.

We had decided to continue pursuing the private adoption when Scott left for a conference in Seattle. However, the next day, I got another phone call from the caseworker. The birthmother had not found anyone with whom she wanted to place her baby.

"This birthmother has two requests. The first is that the adoptive parents must be Protestants. The second is that each of them has at least two years of college. I am having trouble finding a couple like that." Scott was a Protestant minister and we both had master's degrees. "Would you consider an emergency home study and a rush application through the State of Oregon?"

"Of course, but I need to talk to my husband," I answered. Scott and I agreed this was God's leading.

Calling the caseworker back to give our consent, I learned his supervisor had not approved the last-minute rule bending. They were considering several couples as possibilities to present to the birthmother. *Lord, are we hearing you correctly?* In faith, we began filling out the application. Two days later, the supervisor gave permission to go ahead. I mailed in the application papers, aware that some couples had waited two years since filing these items, and had yet to reach this point. *God, is this the miracle you are doing for us?*

Three days later we finished the home study, physicals, and a daylong interview. In a whirlwind, we had covered a process which typically required several months. Then, we were told that on Thursday, March 1st (*my thirtieth birthday!*), the birthmother would make her choice between us and two other families.

Thursday, when the phone rang, I knew this was *the call.*

"The birthmother made her choice this morning," Ed began. I held my breath. "I'm happy to tell you she chose you."

"Oh my gosh, that's great!" I babbled into the receiver.

"The birthmother will be induced Saturday morning."

We called my sister to see if we could borrow newborn clothes, and made plans to spend the night with them before driving to Oregon for the birth. We checked our answering machine when we were at their house on Friday night, and heard Ed's voice, telling us the maternity rooms were full. "The delivery is rescheduled for Monday," he said, before hanging up.

We tried in vain to hold our emotions in check once more as we waited.

Saturday, we headed back home, instead of to the hospital as we had expected. It was a quiet drive, each of us lost in thought and prayer. We punched the answering machine on our way in the door, wondering how we would fill our time until Monday.

"Hi. This is Ed. The birthmother went into labor naturally. She had a healthy baby girl." *Lindsey was here! We were parents of a 9 lb 2 oz. baby girl!*

Ed continued, "By law, the birthmother has twenty-four hours to spend with her baby and consider the decision. You'll have to wait until this period has passed to see the baby."

This means she could change her mind after being with her baby for a whole day. Could we come this close and not receive our baby?

This was the difficult period for Scott. He paced. He

108

Perfect Timing

counted the seconds, the minutes and the hours. I had never seen him so nervous. The anticipation, restlessness and doubt gripped him during this wait. Sleep eluded us both.

Finally, Sunday morning arrived. Never before or since has a three-hour drive taken so long. As we parked the car and hurried toward the hospital, I knew Scott's excitement matched mine. The hallway was cold, colorless and unending. We entered the hospital room where the birthmother and her baby lay.

"I have one request for you," the birthmother said. "Will you please tell her she is adopted?" We assured her it would be no problem for us, as we had already made that decision earlier. We tried to share our hearts with her.

"You cannot know what a gift you have given us. This is a wonderful sacrifice you are making for her. We are so grateful." There was only one message we could convey: "We will love this baby completely, and give her a good home." Our emotions ran high as we left that hospital room, hoping we had adequately expressed our unbounded thankfulness.

Waiting even another few minutes was excruciating. To give the birthmother a chance to say her good-byes, we spent a couple hours out for lunch. When we returned to the hospital, the nurses treated us like we were the birthparents. It felt fantastic. Scott reached in and gently lifted our daughter to eye level. She was beautiful! Our Lindsey, the long awaited answer to our prayers, the child born of our hearts. As we looked into each other's tear-filled eyes, the years of waiting melted away. Holding her, we prayed, "Lord, we want to thank you for this little miracle in our arms. She is more than we could ever have imagined."

My school had no provision for maternity leave for adoptive parents, but graciously allowed me three weeks off to make the adjustments for our baby. Scott, now resigned from his position, was able to be a full-time Daddy. When I returned to work, he cared for Lindsey and bonded with our miracle daughter.

Meanwhile, the pregnant teenager we had heard of previously from Boise Valley Christian Communion was due, and no home had been found yet. We told Pastor Montie about another couple who were hoping for a child, and they became the parents God had planned for that special boy. Soon afterwards, Scott was asked to take a pastoral position at Boise Valley Christian Communion. We gladly accepted that wonderful opportunity.

Still wanting another baby, we sought medical options. Our doctor prescribed fertility pills, but before I could take even one, I became pregnant. We were amazed. I took the pills back and received a refund. Lindsey was a miracle, and this baby was a miracle of equal proportion.

In September, following Lindsey's birth, we finalized her adoption. Afterward we received a letter informing us: "Your application to begin the adoption process has been accepted." The letter went on to say the wait would be at least two years. We read this with our healthy baby in our arms, looked at each other, and smiled at God's timing and provision.

We returned to the California conference that year with one baby in our arms and one on the way. The promise God had given us a year before had more than come true for us. Our son, Travis, was born the following April.

When we dedicated Lindsey on July 8, 1990, a dear woman in our church gave me a Bible scripture ". . .everyone who wants to live a godly life in Christ Jesus will suffer persecution. . . But you must remain faith-

110

ful to the things you have been taught. You know they are true, for you know you can trust those who taught you. You have been taught the Holy Scriptures from childhood, and they have given you the wisdom to receive the salvation that comes by trusting in Christ Jesus." 2 Timothy 3:10-15

This has held true for this child of ours. Lindsey is not bothered by other's opinions, even now, in her teenage years.

She is a beautiful sixteen-year-old, whom people often say looks like her daddy, Scott. With certainty I can say, to our family of four, God has been trustworthy. Both his timing and his plans are perfect.

Chapter 10
Unjustifiable Love
The Story of Ed and Shirley Goff

"Hey, Chris! Come quick!" Mark leaned into the window over the kitchen sink. He strained his eyes to focus on the light in the back room of the house across the street. "There's a light on over at Greg's house! You didn't see them come home early, did you?" Chris jumped sideways over the arm of the recliner he was sitting in. He suddenly came to attention out of his hypnotic state from watching the 10 o'clock news.

"No, they're still out camping. I was just over there to feed the cat on my way home from my mom's house. They won't be back for another day." He spoke while haphazardly grabbing his shoes and ramming his feet into them. He made his way to the window where Mark was, and saw his neighbor's bedroom light glowing. It shone like a beacon against the rest of the blackened house. The way the tiny houses were angled allowed Chris to see through the neighbor's front window and into the back of their house. "Let's go check it out, Mark. No one's getting away with this crap on my watch!"

Mark threw his glass of water into the sink, and the two best friends intuitively agreed to pursue the intruder out of loyalty to their friends. Quickly they crossed the deserted street and slunk into the backyard, careful to not make a sound. This was surreal. Their stealthy, calculated moves were straight out of an action movie. Mark led the way to the back door. Chris followed closely behind him, making sure no one would sneak up on them from behind. He didn't want any surprises. Mark's strategy was to burst in and cause confusion and chaos, hoping to corner whomever had broken in. The white, wooden door had been kicked in and hung loosely from the middle hinge on the doorframe. The splintered wood and the broken doorjamb caused a rage of testosterone to pump through their veins. Chris could hear his pulse in his head against the silence of the night. Caution didn't exist in their minds.

Mark stood six feet tall with broad shoulders. When Chris stood next to him, they looked like Ren and Stimpy. At twenty-two, Chris was 5'8" and only 130 pounds after a heavy meal. He was not at all given to violence, but he had a lion's heart. It roared from within him now.

"What're you doing here?" Mark demanded, as he charged through the kitchen toward the bedroom. Bravery swelled in him. "You're gonna wish you'd never come in here!" he shouted at the shadowy figure.

The intruder pushed his way out of the bedroom, hollering in panic. He knocked Mark down as he ran right through him, then knocked Chris on his rear. Racing through the kitchen, the intruder grabbed a knife from the butcher block and burst through the back door. Mark chased him on foot, and Chris ran back home to get his car.

Five blocks away, Shirley Goff picked up the remains of the bridal shower she had given that night. Everything was quiet now, but the earlier festivities still hung in the air. Suddenly, urgent sirens blared, interrupting her blissful thoughts before they faded. It was a busy traffic area. "Probably just another drag racer getting

114

pulled over," she thought aloud.

The intensity of the chase three neighborhoods away escalated exponentially. "I'm on drugs and I have a knife. If you come at me, I swear I'll kill you!" he threatened Mark. They played cat and mouse, darting here and there through the neighborhood. Chris's car turned the corner, and his headlights caught a silhouette of someone in the distance, one block down. The figure kept looking back as he ran for dear life. "Gotcha!" Chris sneered. He accelerated his '77 Vega towards the perpetrator as the tires picked up dust in the road and created an eerie cloud at the scene. Chris clipped him, but he staggered and regained his balance, then headed toward Maple Grove Road. Out of frustration at the guy's tenacity, Chris was even more determined to capture him. He continued the pursuit on Maple Grove. It was probably just a punk kid that needed to be taught a lesson. If they caught him, maybe he'd be scared enough to never do it again. Chris evened the front end of the car with the burglar, then sped up at the last minute, and angled the car to trap him against a fence. Jumping out of the car, Chris grabbed him. As he did, the burglar's hand jutted forward with a snap, and he thrust the butcher knife into Chris's chest.

Four weeks before, in July of 1979, Ed Goff climbed into bed for the night. He drifted into a vivid, life-like dream. In the dream, Ed was at the Garden City Church he and his family attended. This place was alive with joy and Ed saw himself worshipping wholeheartedly during the Sunday service. Suddenly, the metal roof peeled back and opened to reveal the most beautiful scene he had ever witnessed. Turquoise blue sky, brighter than any oil painting, and enormous white clouds created an arena for Jesus, who stood in their midst. He looked into

Ed's eyes and said in a regally confident yet compassionate tone, "When the earth shakes, be not afraid." Ed stood in awe. It felt as if his hero had come in and dramatically rescued him from a tyrannical bully. Then it was over. But the dream was permanently engraved in his mind. "What was that all about?" he wondered.

That same weekend, Chris invited his mom to go swimming in Idaho City. The two of them stood at the edge of the pristine, blue swimming pool, looking at the reflection of the skyline in the water. "I haven't been swimming in clear water like this for years. All I've done is swim in dirty ditch water!" Chris swung his arms back and forth to gain momentum for his cannonball dive into the water. They floated around lazily, escaping the heat of the noonday sun, laughing and playing like a couple of kids. "All this swimming makes me hungry," Chris announced. High on a grassy hill overlooking Idaho City, they shared their picnic lunch.

"Hey, Mom, there's something I want you to know."

"What's that?" Shirley asked.

"Well, I had an experience not very long ago and I can't tell you about it. All I can say is that it was so frightening, I can't even begin to describe it to you. But I do want you to know this: I am right with myself, I am right with the world, and, most of all, I am right with God." Shirley was glad he had come to a place of peace in his life. "I don't know what the future's going to bring, but I do want you to know that I am right in those areas." Shirley smiled and gently rubbed his hand, basking in the moment.

Mark's legs wouldn't catch up to the rest of his body. He ran full sprint to Chris's car halfway up the driveway. His lungs burned and protested against going any further. He saw two silhouettes in the headlights and then one dropped to the ground. "Chris! Chris!" was all he could say, as he found his friend lying in a pool of blood. No one else was in sight.

"Mark, get me in the car. I'm going to faint," Chris barely whispered.

Terror gripped at Mark's heart and he started screaming, "Help! Help!"

Lights went on in houses, and neighbors poked their heads out their front doors to see what was going on. "Someone call 911!" Mark yelled. The residents of the house stood in stunned silence as Mark saw his friend slipping away. "They're coming, Chris. They're coming right now," Mark reassured his now unconscious friend. The ambulance sirens screamed louder and louder as they approached, emptying a team of paramedics next to Mark and Chris. They began CPR and, in a matter of seconds, Chris was in the ambulance headed for St. Alphonsus Medical Center. The street was eerily silent and normal. The blackness of the night was amplified by the horror of what had taken place. People escaped back into their houses, unsure of what to say or do. Mark spun around in dazed confusion, shaking. Unbelievable. It was totally unbelievable.

"DING-DONG, DING-DONG!" The doorbell rang incessantly. Shirley came out of her deep sleep to find Ed stirring in the dark room, trying to find some clothes. She squinted at the clock on her nightstand, 1:30 a.m. Instinctively, she mentally checked on her children. Both Tracy and Garret are in bed, and Chris was at his place. He had said he was going to go to bed early because he had to get up for his construction job. In her mind, she was putting people in her place while Ed went down the hall to answer the door.

"Don't answer that door! Don't answer that door!" Shirley screamed. A foreboding came over her as the doorbell grew more demanding.

"I have to answer the door, Shirley," Ed said with resignation.

She stood in the doorway of her room in her nightgown, unable to see down the hallway. She listened as Ed opened the door.

"Is this the Goff residence?" A deep male voice came in through the front door.

"Yes," Ed answered.

"Are you Mr. Goff?"

"Yes, yes, what's wrong?" Ed panicked.

"I'm Mr. Madison from the coroner's office and I need to come in and talk to you," the voice said calmly.

It was as if someone had physically punched Shirley. She gasped and grabbed the doorframe to steady herself. The pain was excruciating. She thought, *if I could just pass out, the pain would go away*. The coroner stepped in and they went into the living room.

"Mr. Goff, you need to get Mrs. Goff in here," he directed.

Shirley was standing there down the hall, so she slowly walked around the corner with cheeks drenched from tears and cried, "What's happened to my boy?" She instantly knew this meant tragedy.

"You need to sit down, it's very important that I talk to you," he encouraged her. Tracy and Garret awoke from all the commotion and came from their bedrooms into the living room half asleep.

"What's going on, Dad?" Garret asked.

118

Unjustifiable Love

The coroner stepped in and explained that Chris and his roommate had pursued a burglar in the house across the street they were watching while the neighbors were gone.

"They went over and tried to apprehend the intruder, but he escaped, and Mark chased him on foot, while Chris pursued him in his car. When Chris confronted the man, he stabbed him in his chest through the right ventricle. The paramedics got there within minutes. They thought he had an abdominal wound, not a heart wound, so they did chest compressions to keep his heart going and ended up pumping his blood out. They raced him to the ER where there was a team ready and waiting for him, but as they crossed the threshold of the hospital, he died. There was nothing they could do. I'm so sorry. I wish I could tell you something different. I know this must be such a shock to all of you." The coroner's voice carried his compassion and regret.

And so began the journey of having a loved one's life taken away and the impossible task of forgiveness. After a sleepless night, the Goff family stirred about the house, in shock. *This stuff happens on TV and movies or in L.A., but not in Boise. And certainly not to your own child five blocks from where you live.*

Before breakfast, people were on their doorstep waiting to comfort them. Friends came in droves with words of encouragement and scriptures, many of which had to do with mountains shaking. This was confirmation to Ed that God had tried to comfort him before the murder even happened.

"I don't get it. If God knew ahead of time what would happen, then why would a loving God allow Chris to die like that? He took the trouble of warning you, why

119

didn't he prevent it?" a friend asked.

Ed spoke with quiet strength. "There are people out there who aren't controlled by God and are making decisions. He gives us all free will. God is good. People still do bad things in the world, and he isn't controlling their lives. But in his goodness, he knows how to prepare us and love us through terrible things that are a result of people's bad decisions." Strangely enough, the Goffs brought comfort to their friends as they mourned together the loss of a dearly loved young man.

The next two days passed in a blur of agonizing sorrow. Ed and Shirley laid in bed that morning crying, moaning, and wailing over their loss. The pain was horrible. It was a physical pain that gripped their hearts and overwhelmed them in helpless agony.

"Oh, Chris, I miss you. I miss you. How could this happen? If I could just hold you again... I wish he were here, God. If I could just have him back here, God. It hurts. It hurts so badly." Shirley sobbed uncontrollably. Her chest heaved with great distress. They were exhausted from the intense suffering of grief. Then Ed began to pray. All he knew to do was to forgive. Everything he had learned prior to this told him, the only way to be released from the burden of pain that other people cause you, is to forgive them.

"Dear Jesus, you have promised to be with us through this terrible tragedy. We need you. Shirley, Tracy, Garret and I. God, you forgave us of every wrong thing we've ever done or will do. We also choose to forgive Chris's murderer. Don't let us be swallowed up in bitterness. Now please heal our hearts and hold us in your arms. We can't do this without you. Amen."

There was instant forgiveness in Ed and Shirley's

hearts. Amazingly, there was no animosity or hatred toward the murderer, whoever he was. There was no desire for revenge or a hope that the killer would get what's coming to him. Ongoing sadness? Yes. Anger over the circumstances? Yes. Brokenness? Yes. But hatred? No.

That forgiveness was put to the test in the next year. Two suspects were arrested, brothers, ages nineteen and sixteen. Mark identified the sixteen-year-old in a lineup, and he was then charged with murder. However, Mark, the only eyewitness, was interrogated under hypnosis to alleviate the trauma of recounting that awful night, so his testimony was declared by the state to be invalid. With no other eyewitnesses, there was no case against the two brothers in custody. They were released.

A detective conducted an interview at the home of the sixteen-year-old suspect, where he saw the murder weapon on the table. It was a distinctive knife from the burglarized kitchen. But the detective failed to get a search warrant before going over to the house. When they went back to confiscate it, the knife was gone.

Later, during the pre-investigative hearing, a woman, who lived across the street from Mark and Chris, testified she saw a car parked in front of the burglarized house early on August 9th. Sensing something suspicious, she took down the make and license number of the car. The Judge stopped and looked up abruptly.

"And what was done with that information?"

"Nothing," she replied simply.

The hearing was stopped in order to call the DMV. They looked up the license plate and linked it to the father of the two brothers, placing them at the scene of the crime. But with no eyewitnesses, the case went cold. Their car may have been there and that may prove they burglarized the house, but it didn't prove they committed murder. After incomplete investigations, haphazard prosecution, and no chance of conviction through trial, the reality was that someone killed Chris, and no one was being held accountable for it.

Ed kept busy with his work and maintained his responsibilities on business trips, but there were times when he felt that he could just collapse, mentally and physically. It would have been easy to give in to bitterness over the senseless and careless errors. But Ed made an important decision. "It's okay to be angry, but I don't want it to become who I am."

It took two years for Shirley to finally admit to God just how angry she was and to show her emotions. It swelled in her until it became too great to swallow anymore. Her anger wasn't toward God, she was just mad that it happened and a man chose to stab her child. She was mad that Chris chose to chase an idiot in his car. Mad that the investigation wasn't done correctly. Mad that she had so much pain and that her husband and other two children hurt, too. Mad that life would never be the same again. She felt her muscles tense up and her fingers tightened around the steering wheel of her Chevette. Her heart started pounding and, subconsciously, she held her breath and clenched her jaw. She drove down Maple Grove Road right where Chris was killed. Shirley stopped the car and shook her fist and pounded the steering wheel. "I'm so mad this happened! I wish it had never happened and I want to tell you I'm really, really mad!" She screamed until she was exhausted and hoarse. She cried until her eyes couldn't cry anymore. He already knew, but she got it off her chest.

Shirley drove to a prayer meeting after her fit of

122

anger, where many of her friends asked God to free her from torment. He took away the anger and physical pain in her heart. It was a miraculous transformation. She thought she'd never know what it felt like to be free from a broken heart again. She still felt sadness, but the anger and misery were gone.

Three years went by. One day, Shirley was folding clothes when she had an unexpected understanding. Eighteen months before Chris's death, she had been praying for him. He was a unique young man, full of life and enthusiasm, but he always let himself drift into whatever the crowd was doing. He didn't have any enemies. If the crowd was doing marijuana, he'd do it. If the crowd was wild and crazy drunk, he was too. If they were walking straight, he'd walk straight. If the crowd went to Bible study, he'd go. But he was unable to take what he'd been taught and live by it on his own. So Shirley prayed, "Lord, I'm not praying for this kid one more time until you give me something from your word to stand on." She called a friend and asked her, "Have you ever heard of anything in the Bible that talks about a future or something like that?"

"Yes! That's exactly what Jeremiah 29:11 says, 'I know the plans that I have for you, says the Lord. Plans for your welfare, not for evil. To give you a future and a hope.'"

"That's just what I needed to hear," Shirley said with determination.

Shirley thought back to that time of encouragement.

"But God, I prayed your word and I believed it to be true. What happened?" she asked.

Then she realized that for Chris, his future and

hope was not on earth, but a heavenly one. Three months before he died, she also prayed in desperation, "Oh, Father God, if you know that Chris can never overcome the temptations of the world, I would rather that you take him home to be with you." She knew then, without any doubt, that Chris was where God, in his mercy, had chosen for him to be. He was complete and fully redeemed in heaven. God is good. Even when bad things happen to good people, he is a good God. Shirley had peace of mind. God's grace enabled her and Ed to forgive fully and completely, with the same forgiveness they themselves received in Christ.

Chapter 11
Room for One
The Story of Lee McCormick

Whenever I played this game, I always won. It was a game of Russian Roulette with my virginity. How far could I go without losing it?

"We need to stop." The room felt like it was closing in around me. I was suddenly aware of the stifling closeness, the dampness of the sweat clinging to our bodies, of going too far. "No! Stop!" I had always been capable of stopping the process before. My other boyfriends had been cooperative. This one wasn't.

I tried to will myself to scream or yell, but I was stifled. *I'm the one who agreed to make out*, I chided myself. *You'll make things worse if you make a scene.* I was scared of what he might do if I resisted more strongly. My virginity was gone. The game I played led to great loss, and I grieved. The next school day was excruciating.

Everyone knows. I'm used goods. Nobody will ever want me again, I convinced myself. *I've just got to handle this.* I was familiar with the feeling of having to fend for myself.

My mom and dad divorced when I was three, and I don't ever remember them being together. It was normal to have a mom and dad that were not married.

I saw my dad every other weekend, but nothing was stable. There always seemed to be a new wife or girlfriend in his life. I lived with my mom, but we ended up moving a lot. My hunger for God conflicted with my decision to shut him out. This tore me apart. I felt like I was living in two different worlds. One Sunday, I prayed, "God, this is too hard. I live one way at school and a different way at church. I can't do it anymore. I can't be two-faced to you. I'm just going to live my own life. I'm not going to live for you, it's too hard." I turned my back on God and put both feet on the other side of the fence. The pressure was off.

By the time I was fifteen, I felt I needed to take control. I knew I'd have much less supervision at my dad's house. "I want to go and live with Dad," I announced one day. I could see from the color in Mom's face that those words hurt deeply.

"You do?" Mom tried to hold her voice steady.

I needed a solid foundation. I needed to know something was going to stay the same, or at least feel like it would stay the same. The one speck of security I derived from my dad was that he always lived in the same house. If the relationships in my life couldn't be permanent, the location could be a solid spot on which to land.

My mom bought a house shortly after I moved in with Dad. Her house always felt more like home. Time spent at my dad's house was not as nurturing, because the current woman in his life was the center of his attention. I was more of a background fixture. My dad's basement became my own private bachelorette pad. If I stayed out of his way, he stayed out of mine. My mom invited me to go to church with her, and occasionally I did, but I was still living in two worlds.

I started smoking pot when I was still living with my mom, but her strictness kept it in check. There were no such constraints after I moved in with my dad. My older brother and I started experimenting with cigarettes, which led to experimenting with liquor and getting drunk, which led to smoking pot on a regular basis.

Through ninth grade, my brother had been the male figure in my life, my trusted confidant. But now he was leaving for the Navy. It left one more hole in my heart. *I'm all alone,* I thought. I wondered how I would survive without my big brother to lean on.

In my sophomore year, I started dating a pothead. *I can change him,* I reasoned. *I will save him from himself.* His problems gave me something else to focus on, instead of my own purposelessness. This tactic was only temporarily effective. Eventually, we broke up and I dated a bunch of guys. The never-ending search to fill the emptiness with sexual games proceeded at a rapid pace.

The summer before my junior year of high school, I put myself, as I had many times before, in a risky situation. I lost at Russian Roulette, and was forced to have sex against my will; I wasn't strong enough to stop it. Our relationship became destructive from that point on. I continued having sex in order to anesthetize my pain. The initial high I gained after every encounter, however, was not worth the downward spiral into guilt that always followed. I was afraid to take a real look at my life, so I validated my actions by keeping the status quo. I told myself, *if I keep giving out, he will honor me in time.* I was just lying to myself. We broke up after several months.

Who am I fooling? This is stupid. I knew somewhere in the depths of my existence that my answer was in God. *How can I get back to God now, after I've thrown everything in his face for so long?* Within a few Sundays, I returned to church. That particular Sunday, the high school group was praying for young women who had given their hearts away to guys and had been hurt. Denice Cain prayed for me and, for the first time in a long time, I felt I was worth something to God.

My heart was broken. Acknowledging what I had done wrong was the beginning of healing. I went home to my dad's house and cried out to God, "Why did I turn my back on you and play these games? It was so stupid." God had initiated the major surgery required for me to be whole again. It was painful, but with this first cut, the pus of anger and bitterness began to seep out of my inner parts. Coming back to God proved to be a slow process.

I continued in this same self-destructive lifestyle through the rest of high school and into college. Smoking pot in my dad's basement was normal. I had two friends who were cohorts in this habit. We smoked all the time, before school, at lunch break, and anytime we could squeeze in a joint. We'd get stoned, watch TV, eat and go on hikes. We bought mass quantities of pot so we wouldn't have to go hunting for some every time we wanted to get high. Thousands of dollars literally went up in smoke.

Walking on campus one day shortly after school started, a girl stopped me. "Hey, would you like to study the Bible with me?"

"Okay. Sure. Whatever." I didn't even know why I was saying yes. We exchanged phone numbers.

"Cool, I'll see you Saturday," she said as she walked away.

I called my mom. "Hey, guess what?"

"What?" Mom always seemed ready to listen to me.

"Some girl invited me to study the Bible with her. I'm thinking of going, isn't that weird?"

"That's great!" Mom told me that she had been

praying for me to get into the Bible. My mom knew that prayer changes things. She continually talked to God about me, asking for my safety and that I would find my way back to my relationship with the one who loved me most.

I did go the Bible study. *Man, I'm just using God for whatever I can get. I'm not really living for him*, I thought.

I knew this was true because one night, when I was alone, fear filled my downstairs bedroom. I felt a dark presence and an overwhelming fear, a paralyzing fear. My only defense was to pull the covers over my head. When I told Mom about it she said, "Lee, you have asked Jesus into your heart and if you tell that thing to go away in Jesus' name, it will go away." I knew she was right.

The next night, I felt that dark presence again, and I simply said, "You get out of my room in Jesus' name and don't ever come back!" The darkness that had inhabited my room left, and never came back. The hard, callous cover of my heart developed a small fissure.

After the second Bible study meeting, I decided, *I'm tired of playing games with God. I want to live the way he wants me to live.* I went out to the car and told God, "Okay, God, this is my last cigarette. We're going to smoke this last cigarette and then I'm done." And I was. I've never smoked another one. It's hard sometimes, even more than three years later. I just have to keep saying, "No."

I opened up to God, studied the Bible with my friends, and determined that I was going to stop doing all the things God didn't want me to do.

"I've got to get right with Jesus, and these are the five things I'm going to quit doing: I'm going to quit smoking cigarettes, I'm going to quit having sex with this guy, I'm going to quit swearing, I'm going to quit drinking, and I'm going to quit smoking pot." I ticked these off on my fingers. Pot was last on the list, because I knew it would be the hardest one to kick. By the strength of my willpower, I would prove to God I was capable of living for him.

Shortly after that, I headed for a church retreat. I got stoned on the way up the mountain to the retreat. The sharp curves of Bogus Basin Road flowed underneath the tires of my car. At this season in my life, being sober was abnormal. Miraculously, I arrived safely at the meeting place.

After the sermon that night, we all sat on the bed chatting.

"You know what," I said, the words tumbling out of my mouth, "I'm a huge, fat, pothead. I got stoned on the way up here. I've been trying to act like my life's all together. I've been struggling all night not to swear around you so you'd think my life was okay, but it's not. I've been smoking pot every day for five years, and I don't care."

The words kept coming. I told them about a sexual relationship I was having with an older man. It was all about the sex, and there really was nothing more to the relationship. Each time, I would think, *this has to be the last time; this is stupid.* As a matter of fact, it made my skin crawl to be in his place. Validation, acceptance, even though it's negative, can be such a tremendous pull. It made me do things I detested. The void left by my brother's departure, and Dad's preoccupation with the women in his life, still screamed to be filled.

Instead of judging me, these friends seemed to understand, and most importantly, they offered a way out.

130

Room For One

"Are you ready to make a decision to let God help in these situations?"

Before I could give it a second thought, I said, "Yes. It's way too hard to quit smoking pot all by myself. I can't do it by myself. Jesus, you've got to help me out here." I decided that night that I was going to live for God. Freedom was at hand.

"Thank you, Lord, for setting me free," I burst out. "Thank you for setting me free from unhealthy relationships, and from pot... from the false god of pot. I am so sorry I missed the target. I want to do what you have for me to do." I had used pot as my backbone, something to fall back on, a way to gain strength. Now God was my backbone, the one person I would depend on to be my strength. That night, God took every craving for pot away from me. I never wanted it again.

The next day, the girls came over and we smashed all my drug paraphernalia and flushed hundreds of dollars of pot down the toilet. Difficult would be a good description of these activities, but I knew if I didn't do it now, I wouldn't do it. I couldn't continue to serve two gods.

"You know, you've got to call that guy and tell him it is over." My friends' words registered loud and clear. I decided to wait until he called me. I had a script written, so I would know exactly what to say to him.

One night, the phone rang. I knew the fear was evident in my voice, but I told him firmly, "I can't see you any longer. We can't do what we're doing; this is wrong. I've given my life to Jesus. This is goodbye." I never spoke to him again. The messages he left on subsequent occasions made me so thankful that God helped me get out of that relationship.

I grew close to my mom and my stepdad. Support

and encouragement met me at the door every time I went to their home. They were so proud of me and of the new turn my life had taken. My stepdad, and some of the pastors from my church, baptized me in my mom's swimming pool. That is one of the top five days of my life. There's only room for one God in my life, now. I have moved forward with him, and I no longer look for my identity in a man. I know how much I am worth in Christ.

God does, too, and he erased all the shame of my life. He sent me a husband who treasures me. God pursued me with his amazing love and resolve, and I have chosen to follow him, and him alone.

Chapter 12
Course Change
The Story of Matt Hyde

The drive through LaPlata Canyon never failed to amaze me. My dog, Mojo, and I drove between towering peaks, which eventually emptied into a plateau. I lost all track of time. Parking my truck in a notch of the canyon, I took a hit from my pipe, exhaled, and breathed in the beauty of my surroundings.

On one side lay the whole San Juan Valley, Durango at its foot, with the San Juan Mountains off in the distance. Behind me, stood the LaPlata Mountains in their entire splendor. As Mojo explored the rocky sprawl, I took another hit.

Phaa-room! Thunder bellowed through the wind like a deep, angry whisper. I started climbing to the peak, several hundred feet above me. Looking out toward the San Juan Mountains, I could see black thunderclouds starting to engulf the valley. Emptiness crushed me. *What am I doing here?* I wondered, as black thunderclouds inched their way closer to the valley below. My dismal self-pity matched the darkening sky, and sorrow welled up inside of me. As rain started to fall, so did my tears.

Ka-boom! Closer now, the thunder roared across the peaks adjacent to me. It was not a wise idea to be standing twelve thousand feet high at that particular moment. *Who cares if I get hit by lightning?* I thought as my self-pity grew. *What do I have to look forward to?* Flash... Ka-boom! A thunderbolt tagged the ground not too far from me. "That's right, what do I have to live for?" I shouted. "Go ahead, take my life!" I screamed. The rain was really coming down now, camouflaging my tears. Flash... Kaboom! Another bolt of lightning hit the valley floor just below me. I raised my fists to the sky, shook them, and shouted, "You are a coward, God, if you won't take my life right now! What do you want from me?" Flash... Kaboom! Another bolt touched down very close to me.

I wiped the flood of tears and rain from my eyes, and looked down to see my dog cowering at my feet. Mojo looked up at me as if to say, "I care." Never in my life had I felt so drained, so emptied, with nothing more to give. Lightning and thunder were all around us, as Mojo whimpered, shaking in fear. *Was there any reason for me to live?*

It wasn't like me to be suicidal or even depressed. Growing up in Big Sky, Montana and Eagle, Idaho, I had a typical, middle class childhood. I loved to ski and play soccer. It wasn't until I started high school that my life took a downturn. My parents sent me to a private, church-run school. It was very odd for me. This seemed like a cold, regimented religion. I hated it, and I had no desire to become a member of that religion or a follower of God. I did, however, enjoy going to parties and drinking with my buddies. The school had only so much control over us.

After graduation, I attended Fort Lewis College in Durango, Colorado. I was thrilled to play soccer in a Division II school, and red-shirted my freshman year. It should have been a high point in my life, but partying was very much a part of the soccer team's culture. There wasn't a day, from the beginning of the semester until Thanksgiving break, that I was sober. This took its toll

134

Course Change

on my studies. My grade point average for the first semester was an embarrassing 1.6.

As Christmas break approached, my mother called. I was getting high with my roommates and didn't feel like talking to her. I became very belligerent and argumentative with her on the phone. Then she dropped the sledgehammer on me.

"Andrew was in a car wreck coming home from university," she bolted out in a very angry tone. "He was hit head-on by a semi truck and is in the hospital in critical condition."

Andrew was my best friend when I was growing up in Big Sky. He is one of those rare people who truly cared about others. That made the news hard for me to hear. He was such a nice guy and so sincere. *Why did this have to happen to him?* My bitterness only increased over the Christmas break.

In the second semester of school, I started doing methamphetamines and cocaine. I was stuck in a vicious whirlpool, a vortex that was sucking me deeper and deeper into a black hole. My life seemed to be veering off course, but I had no idea which direction I needed to go. Unfortunately, life got worse before it got better.

After finally graduating from college, I worked for Southwest Youth Corps as the crew boss, overseeing twelve men. Our job was to work with different forest personnel on forest thinning projects. The pay was good, and I loved the work. Unfortunately, we were drinking, smoking pot, and often putting our lives in danger. It was incredibly reckless, since I was responsible for the crew and their safety. I made some of the poorest decisions in my life on that job, and ended up getting fired. Then I met a guy named Brad, and the two of us decided to start a business in Montana.

Brad and I had no place to stay when we got to Montana. All of our stuff was in the back of my truck. Brad didn't have anything, so we lived on the money in my bank account. Andrew had recovered well from his accident and was back at university. Since we didn't have a place to stay, Andrew's mom, Darlene, opened up her house to us so we could take showers and get cleaned up. While we were there, Brad and I rummaged around the house and found stashes of money and alcohol that somehow we felt entitled to. I justified taking it by saying that Darlene would have given me the money, had I asked. She was that kind of person.

A friend of mine owned a landscaping business, and hired us to work for him. It was temporary, and we earned just enough money to feed ourselves and buy alcohol. We eventually stole a chainsaw from him so that we would have two of them for our own business.

After awhile, we started working for some friends who owned a ranch just outside of Butte. We lived on the ranch for about a month, while we cleared trees on their property for cross-country skiing. I didn't have the money for my truck registration, so we stole the license plates off of one of their trucks. This was one way to make my truck legal, sort of.

It was around this time that I started feeling suspicious about Brad. I knew he tended to stretch the truth, but his stories were starting to go way overboard. *Has he ever really been honest with me?* I started feeling uneasy about him, and at times, I was a little scared.

"If anyone ever crosses me, I will kill him!" he said. "If anyone ever hurts my son, I'll hunt them down." It sounded like Brad was not right in the head, maybe a

Course Change

little crazy. I started thinking, *I need to get away from this guy.*

On a trip to Idaho Falls, I met some of Brad's friends who confirmed my growing suspicions. Bam! My eyes were opened. Now, I was really spooked. I needed to find a way to get away from Brad, which included getting everything out of storage in Big Sky.

While we were still in Idaho Falls, Brad had to go out on a job for the day. It was my chance. I headed for the storage shed in Montana.

"What the heck?" I couldn't believe it. "Where's my stuff?" I said to no one in particular. Everything was gone. I found out Brad had convinced a friend to empty out the shed of what he claimed was his stuff. When we found Brad's friend in Butte, she was skeptical.

"I can tell you exactly what is in there," I claimed. "The trunk was my mother's, and has all of my papers and journals in it." It took a while, but eventually I convinced her. In a flash, I loaded it into my truck and took off. As I was heading out of town, I saw Brad in a car and knew he would follow me.

Somewhere down the road, I called my parents. I had no money for gas, and I felt they needed to know what was happening. My mom was frantic.

"The police called here asking questions about you. Brad said you stole some things from him!" My parents were both upset. "What's going on, Matthew?" my dad blurted out.

"What? He's crazy! He's after me, he tried to steal all of *my* stuff!" I countered.

"Brad claims you stole all of *his* stuff," my mom finished. She wasn't even trying to keep her voice calm.

I let out a few choice words. I didn't know if Brad had told the police about the stolen license plates or not.

137

Dread turned to fear. With few other options, I headed to a nearby police station. I told them the truth about the stuff in the back of my truck. I gave the police the few things that weren't mine, but I lied to them about Brad's gun. When the police asked me about the gun, I told them I didn't know anything about it. Actually, I gave the gun to someone to throw into the river, because I didn't want Brad to have it.

After the stop at the police station, I headed for my parents' house in Boise. As soon as I got home, I called the people whose license plates I had stolen and confessed my crime. The next day, I packaged up the plates and mailed them back. I was half out of my mind worrying about what would happen next. My own shadow frightened me.

I started contacting my old friends and they welcomed me with open arms. We immediately started partying again and, not realizing it, I became more lost than ever. Back to my self-destructive pattern, my fears subsided. After a few drinks and a couple of parties, nothing seemed to matter.

I found comfort while talking with my longtime friend, Monica. Throughout my travels with Brad, I had called her. She and I were from two different worlds, but somehow our differences drew us closer. Our conversations grew in intensity and we started dating. Monica's stubborn refusal to be in a relationship with me as long as I was a heavy drug user, inspired me. I decided to leave my party buddies behind. *This life is getting me nowhere, I gotta get out of here.* I was ready to change. Eventually, Monica and I moved in together. It must have been hard for Monica. She stuffed her former convictions, and continued going to church all the while she was living with

138

Course Change

me. One day, I asked her, "Could you ever marry someone with different beliefs?"

"No, I absolutely could not." Her stark answer stunned me. Yet somehow I understood. Monica's whole family was into God, even her little niece, Alexia.

When Alexia was about four, Monica and I were invited to "family night" at Monica's sister's house. Alexia procrastinated going to bed, as most children do, and her ploy was to have each of us come in, one by one, to say goodnight to her.

"Send Matt next," Alexia instructed. I thought it was cool that she included me.

"Good night, Alexia," I said, after a hug.

"You can't leave. You have to pray with me," she stated.

I knew I couldn't fake something that I had no experience in. So I looked her in the eye and told her the truth. "I don't know how to pray, but Aunt Monica is teaching me."

The puzzled look on her face was less than comforting. I was never so relieved to get out of there. It hit me hard. I only knew rote church prayers, not how to talk straight to God. When I came out of Alexia's room, everyone was enjoying a laugh at my expense.

The next week, when bedtime rolled around, I thought, *Great! Alexia's going to call me in again and she's gonna ask me to pray!* I had no idea what I would tell her. I couldn't give her the I-don't-know-how excuse again. That was a one-time only reprieve, especially with this sharp four-year-old. Sure enough, she called for me like a princess-in-waiting, and there I was.

"Are you gonna pray with me tonight, Matt?" I knew it was coming.

"I don't think I can. Um, Aunt Monica is still teaching me how to pray," I stumbled. *Who can lie to a four-year-old?*

"I'll show you how. Just say what I say," Alexia assured me. So I did. I repeated every word Alexia prayed.

When we were living together, Monica got up early every Sunday and left quietly for church, while I lay in bed. My curiosity began to grow and I wondered what her church, Boise Valley Christian Communion, was like. She finally invited me, but, once inside, I was very uncomfortable. Everyone wanted to know who the guy was with the pastor's daughter. I didn't go back for a couple weeks.

Then, one Sunday morning, as usual, Monica got up early and left quietly. This time, the minute she stepped out the door, I jumped up, dressed, and headed for her church. I spotted Monica toward the front of the sanctuary, singing and clapping her hands to the music along with everyone else. When she turned around and saw me, it was as if time stood still. I felt like I was supposed to be there, but it still made me uneasy.

I kept going back, and a few weeks later, Daniel and Betty Wilmot invited Monica and me to lunch after church. After we chatted, they invited me to a small group later that night. I was skeptical, but uncontrollably intrigued and drawn to it.

That evening, I kissed Monica goodbye and headed out. When I arrived at the house, I could see through the front window. There were people sitting around the living room. I continued walking toward the door, even though I couldn't feel my legs moving. Nervously, I considered heading back to the car, when the front door opened. "Hi, Matt. Welcome," Daniel said.

140

Course Change

Oops, too late. No turning back now, I thought. So in I went.

That night, a woman named Debbie, who I figured must be a regular there, started telling her life story. She talked about her childhood and all the problems she had growing up. Then she talked about how Jesus had come into her life. How he had set her free and wiped away everything that had weighted her down since childhood. "And now," she said, "I have an abundance of joy in the morning when I wake up, wondering what God has in store for me this day."

My eyes were wide open. It felt like my jaw had dropped onto my lap. I was in awe when I left this small group of people. Up to this point, I had thought Christians were a bunch of hypocrites: confessing their sins, asking for forgiveness, then going out and committing the same sins over again. I thought religion was a way to justify their immoral lifestyles. After all, this was what we did at the church-run high school. But hearing this woman speak about Jesus changed my whole attitude about Christianity.

When I got home, Monica looked at me, and in a very reserved voice, asked, "Hey, how are you doing?" I then proceeded to tell her about the meeting. *It's great to hear Christians being so honest about life*, I thought, as I remembered Debbie's story. Later that evening, we took our dogs for a walk on the greenbelt.

At one point, I stopped and, not realizing what I was saying, I blurted out, "Hey, I think I let Jesus into my heart."

Monica paused in mid-step. "What did you say?"

"I don't know. Wow. I think I let Jesus into my heart!" We were both amazed by those simple words that slipped out of my mouth. I felt changed in a way I couldn't explain. I didn't really understand what had happened. All I knew was that I was different.

After that, things started changing quickly. Daniel and I met on a regular basis, and he helped make sense out of all that had happened to me. I understood that being a Christian was a powerful, life-changing commitment. Monica and I quit living together, and moved home with our respective parents. I learned that repenting of my sins also required restitution, and that God was all about restoring relationships.

When I told Daniel about all the stuff I had stolen from Darlene in Montana, he said I had to make that right. I had to pay her back the money I had stolen, plus interest. I thought, *No way am I doing that.* I told Daniel I would have to think about that one.

Living with Monica had also damaged our relationship with her parents. I started hanging around them and began tearing down the walls that we had created. Eventually, I wanted to ask Monica to marry me, but before I could do that, I knew God wanted me to repair the damage I had created with her parents. I told them I was sorry for living with Monica, and asked them to forgive me. Wow! When they forgave, God poured his grace out on me and it was unlike anything I had ever felt before. The wounds I had created in Monica's parents began to heal, too. We were married soon thereafter.

Darlene came to the wedding and I had a hard time facing her. When we opened Darlene's wedding gift and found a hundred dollars for our honeymoon, my heart was torn. I knew then what I needed to do. When Monica and I returned from our honeymoon, my mother told me that Darlene had had a stroke. *If something happens to her before I can ask her forgiveness, I don't think I can live with myself,* I thought.

I tried to call Darlene, but could not get through to her. Then I wrote her a five-page letter, confessing my theft and asking for her forgiveness. Tears flowed as I wrote. Perhaps my actions had destroyed my relationship with Andrew and his mother. To make restitution, I bought a bank draft check and included it in the letter. A month later the bank called and said they were going to cancel the check unless it was cashed soon. My heart sank. I convinced myself that Darlene hated me for what I had done. I called her several more times and left messages, but didn't hear from her. I was sick with the thought that she may never forgive me. One day, I finally called when she was home and she apologized for not getting back to me.

"I'm not going to cash the check, Matt. I'm sending it back to you." I didn't know what to say. "Sounds like you were in a horrible place back then. I'm so happy that you're getting your life together and that you've found God."

"I'm glad, too."

"You are very brave to call and write to me about what happened." She assured me she had forgiven me for taking the money. Then, she ended by saying, "I'm proud of you, Matt."

I lost it. Uncontrollable tears flowed. Never in my whole life had I felt so thankful and so complete than when I got off the phone with Darlene that day. My heart was restored in a way I never imagined possible.

God performed miracles in my life. What an amazing opportunity I've had to repair damage done in relationships and to learn to know God. He's no coward after all. He has healed the scars from the depressing and pathetic life I once lived. I am no longer lost, no longer depressed and I really do know which way to go from here.

Chapter 13
Wild Joy
The Story of Rhonda Willoughby

I awoke with a start, the troublesome thought once again wedging its way into my consciousness. *Could I be pregnant? No, impossible! After all, I'm only fifteen. I have a biology test coming up. Surely, I'm just messed up in my cycle.* A few months later, however, I could no longer deny the obvious. The butterfly flutters were becoming stronger everyday, and none of my friends had skipped four periods in a row.

I lived in fear. How was I going to tell my parents, and when? Paralyzing thoughts brought a dark cloud of loneliness over me. There was no one to help shoulder the agony. I couldn't share this with a friend, and I had no idea who the father might be.

On the outside, I pretended that everything was normal, laughing with friends, trudging the halls from class to class. On the inside, however, I tried out every possible scenario as I planned the moment of disclosure. I finally settled on telling my mom after dad had gone to his 24-hour work shift. Perhaps she could soften the blow. Maybe he would cool down before he got home.

His truck had no more than pulled out of the driveway, when I began looking for the perfect moment. Once I was sure my younger brother was out of the house, I approached Mom. The well-crafted speech failed me; bluntly, my words spilled from the floodgate of weeks of pent-up worry. Her expression went from shock to fear to anger, all within seconds.

"You're what?" she shouted, then burst into tears. Hands trembling, she picked up the phone and dialed my dad while I numbly stood by, unable to utter another word. I listened as she reported my news. Apparently he had plenty to say, judging by the long pause in her conversation. Slowly, she placed the phone back on the cradle. Shoulders sagging, her eyes locked on mine. "He's coming home now," she said.

Fear grabbed me once again. Withdrawing to my room, I awaited the inevitable confrontation. Doubtless he would be angry; so much for the cool down I had secretly hoped would occur.

Gravel flew as he pulled up in front of the house. I heard the door slam and his voice shouting, "Where is she?" Somehow I mustered enough courage to face him. I had never seen him this angry. Raging, he forced me to kneel before him, slapping me in the process. "Slut, whore, bitch...," his defining words, degrading words, tore through my mind. I was no longer worthy of being called his daughter. The verdict had been given. Then came the decree.

"We will take care of this," my father boomed. "You are not having this baby. No one will know you were pregnant. You will have an abortion immediately!" No one ever questioned my father's authority. His words were final. Fearing him as I did, I knew I had no options; any thoughts of the baby were completely overshadowed.

What had brought me to this devastation? Bad choices, to be sure, but seeds were planted long before, when I was an impressionable five-year-old. My parents, together with my brother and I, went to a nudist camp in the mountains near Boise. Although sexual activity was not supposed to occur, it didn't take long for inquisitive children to wander into the bushes and engage in sexual experimentation with the older children. These outings occurred until I was about ten. In addition, my parents had friends come to our home for nude parties. Neighborhood children peeked through cracks in our fence, spying out the gatherings. Later, their taunts and jeers embarrassed me.

By the time I was thirteen, I was sexually active with boys my age. I started driving at fourteen and had my own car when I was fifteen. Having no curfew, I often stayed out until 2 or 3 a.m. In addition to random sex, my friends and I also drank and used drugs, never thinking of the consequences beyond the next high. My abundant freedom came with a price, however.

Within a couple of weeks following my disclosure, Mom took me to the hospital for the abortion. Since I was more than five months pregnant, the doctor induced labor. My mom sat at my bedside throughout the process. Dad was absent. I was one frightened girl in a sea of stainless steel and pain. Like everything around me, any interaction with the doctor or nurses was sterile—void of kindness or cruelty. After six hours of contractions, I finally delivered. Although I was awake, I did not see the baby or know its gender.

We returned home shortly after the delivery. Dad spoke to me only when absolutely necessary. The events of the day were neatly stashed into the family "no discussion" box. Life was supposed to resume, with my pregnancy being only a blip on the screen. I returned to school and tried to forget, but I couldn't shake the feelings of shame and guilt. With resounding clarity, I knew

I had killed a person.

Consequently, I tried to anesthetize myself. I increased previous destructive behaviors of partying, drugs and sex. Two years later, shortly following graduation, I was pregnant again. This time there was no family meeting. My fiancé, Dave, and I planned our wedding and were married in October.

As soon as my father deduced I was pregnant before our marriage, there was no more contact from him. In April our daughter was born, and we named her Christina. Overshadowing my happiness, however, was my father's refusal to see me or the baby.

Although I abstained from drinking while pregnant, I resumed partying once the baby was born. Within five years, our home became a battleground. My husband wanted me at home all the time, cleaning and caring for our daughter. His control and my rebellion were not a formula for a happy marriage. Like a caged animal, I was looking for an escape and found it by having a brief affair. I ended it within three weeks, and hit an all time low. I was so tired—tired of drinking, tired of marijuana, tired of cocaine, and tired of living.

During one of our many fights, I dropped a word bomb and told Dave about the affair. Doubling up his fist, he punched a hole in the wall.

"I'm done," I retorted. "Christina, pack your bags, we're leaving!" Although I knew my confession had caused his angry display, I was devoid of feeling. My empty threat hung in the air. Somehow we made it through that night, with Dave on the couch and me in our bed. In spite of my indiscretion, Dave did not want a divorce.

The next morning, I awoke with one thought:

Wild Joy

Pastor Tom. Tom Blackburn, pastor of Community Christian Center in Garden City, was an icon to everyone who lived there. I had met him once during my teens, but that meeting was foggy at best because I was intoxicated at the time. However, I knew he had established a youth center to provide a place for young people to get off the streets, and he often helped feed the poor. Perhaps he would be able to help me, too. In desperation, I drove to the church.

What am I doing? I wondered halfway there. *Has he ever heard a story like mine? How much do I dare tell him?* These questions weakened my resolve. However, my pain was greater than my fear. *What have I got to lose?* I argued as I pulled into the church parking lot.

Pastor Tom greeted me as I entered the church. After brief introductions, I cautiously told him how frustrated I was with my life.

"We're having a meeting at the church tonight. Why don't you come?" he suggested. I was willing to try anything, so I accepted his invitation.

Sitting at a table in the fellowship hall, the evangelist asked, "May I ask what led you here to seek us out?"

"I'm here because I'm in trouble," I began as tears welled up. I was a bit surprised at how close my emotions were to the surface, and how willing I was to talk to this stranger. I then proceeded to pour out my story.

"Rhonda, God is able to put broken lives back together," the evangelist gently explained. "Does that sound like something you would like to know more about?"

With tears, I eagerly nodded. "I've made so many mistakes, though. Seems to me God would rather wipe

149

me out than fix me," I cried.

"Our mistakes are called sin, Rhonda, and sin keeps us away from God. But in his love, God created a plan to bring us back. His son, Jesus, offers us forgiveness and new life. It is available to you right now."

It sounded almost too good to be true! "I'm more than ready," I willingly replied.

Humbly, I prayed as the evangelist led me. "Lord Jesus, please forgive me for my sins and come into my heart." These simple but powerful words brought peace to me like I had never known. I felt clean and pure, like a huge weight had been lifted from my shoulders. Joy started bubbling up in me.

From that day on, I jumped in with both feet, attending church with Christina. I was starving to get to know God better. I prayed daily and devoured chapters in my new Bible.

Although Dave and I started seeing a marriage counselor right away, he did not get involved with my newfound faith for almost a year. "Church again?" he'd say. "You're trying to turn everything into a prayer meeting." In spite of the ridicule, I was content. Gradually, Dave's heart began to soften. He started attending Christian parties and later told me he had accepted Jesus as his Savior years ago. Eventually, he came to church with Christina and me on Sunday mornings. The healing of our marriage had started.

During that first year, God also began healing my heart. I met Millie Williams, who became my friend. She sensed I was carrying emotional wounds that needed healing.

One day as we talked over tea and Pepsi, she showed me a new book she had recently read. "It's about inner healing," she said. "I think some of these principles may help you deal with the hurts of your past. Are you interested?"

I nodded, not fully understanding what she was suggesting. Together we read some of the passages from the book. As we talked further, I shared secrets I had hidden in the dark corners of my heart.

"I've never prayed with anyone like this, but I'm willing if you are," she said.

"Let's give it a try," I replied, trusting her completely. We moved into the living room, choosing the floor instead of chairs. "Dear God, please show me those I need to forgive," I began. Clutching Millie's hand tightly, I agreed with God and forgave my mom and dad, my brother, the doctor, my husband, and myself. Together we walked back through the years, as God brought to my remembrance others I needed to forgive and events from which I needed cleansing. I was now free to see my parents with new eyes.

Over the next few years, Dave and I continued to work on our marriage and our spiritual growth. I taught Sunday school to preschoolers, learning the Bible stories along with the children. Most Sundays we were in church. My dad remained indifferent, but my mom became curious.

"How do you know you will go to heaven?" Mom asked one day as we were driving down the road. This was the opening I needed.

"I know because the Bible says if we accept Jesus as our Savior, we will live with him eternally. He forgives and accepts us if we turn to him," I replied. I then had the awesome joy of leading my mom in the prayer of salvation, just as I had prayed.

In 1988, an evangelist, Tommy Hawks, came to our church for revival meetings. Dave and I had a spare bedroom in our home and invited Tommy to be our houseguest. At home, following one of the meetings, I was smoking a cigarette before going to bed. Suddenly God spoke to my spirit, "You don't want those anymore."

Crushing the cigarette, I asked Tommy, "Will you pray for me? I believe God just showed me that I really don't need these anymore."

Tommy readily complied, and God answered the prayer. Although I had been smoking a pack to a pack and a half a day, I never had another one from that night on. God completely removed the craving.

For the next ten years, I continued to pray for my family. Although I was stronger emotionally and spiritually, one area of contention remained: my father. Long after my marriage, he still had the ability to control me by his raging. Then one day, during a siege, I drew boundaries. "No, Dad, you will not do this any longer," I declared, surprising myself almost as much as him. In stunned silence he retreated. No one in our family had ever stood up to him before.

When Christina was barely eighteen, she became pregnant. Together we sat down and discussed her options. Abortion was not one of them. I disclosed the heartache of my abortion, but mainly focused on her choices—adoption versus keeping the baby and raising it as a single mom.

Dave and I sent her to a counselor, making it clear that we would not be raising this child, should she decide to keep it, but that we would fully support her decision. She ultimately decided to keep her baby.

My next step was to tell my parents. Amid memories of my own first pregnancy, I prayed for God's help. I called my dad and simply told him Christina was pregnant. "If you cannot say anything kind or positive to her, you will not say anything at all," I warned. "We are supporting our daughter." I breathed a sigh of relief that I had already learned to stand up to him.

That December, Christina delivered a beautiful baby girl, Alexandria. We were delighted with our new granddaughter and sent a video to my parents. A month later they returned from their annual winter trip, and came directly to the house to meet the newest family member. Without hesitation, Dad asked to hold the baby. Gently, he cradled Alexandria in his arms, and as he held her, I saw a transformation begin. It was nearly four hours later that he finally relinquished his hold and allowed someone else to take her. That sweet, tiny baby had melted her great-grandfather's heart!

Several years later my parents, now accustomed to our church attendance, decided to come with us. During worship I felt a nudge from God. "Today is the day for your dad, Rhonda."

Following the sermon, Pastor Tom invited us to take communion. Dad stood at the back of the church and God spoke to my heart. "Go back there." Obediently, I complied.

"Dad, I have to ask you a question," I quietly pressed.

"What?" he returned.

"I need to know if you believe that the Lord Jesus Christ is your Lord and Savior."

"Yes, I do," he replied, looking intently at me.

"Will you come and take communion with me?" Together we walked down the center aisle. Stillness settled over the room. People who had prayed with me those many years recognized my father was making his declaration.

Today I stand in awe of my incredible God, who has been so faithful to my whole family. It has been thirty-two years since the abortion. I believe someday I will see my child in heaven. Meanwhile, my daughter is a happily married mom who loves God and is teaching her children to love him. My parents are attending a church where they are growing in their faith. My husband and I are blessed in our marriage, and serve God together at Boise Valley Christian Communion.

I know the importance of forgiveness. The Bible says, "If we confess our sins, he is faithful and just and will forgive us our sins and purify us from all unrighteousness." I John 1:9 (NIV) I asked him to forgive me, and I know he has. He enabled me to forgive others. God has restored my relationships and given me joy.

154

Afterthoughts

I hope you enjoyed reading these stories as much as I did. Remember, I know these people and their stories; however, I never cease to be amazed by their transparency. We hope that as you read this book, you could identify with the stories here, and see that you, too, can be changed. These are real people who worship with us every week. When we began this project, Cindy Anderson, our Project Manager, said it best: "I am undone. As I read through the first set of testimony surveys submitted, I am humbled, for I see clearly that, every week, I worship among heroes of the faith. I am in awe. We should gladly rub elbows with each other more closely as a body, because the people sitting beside us carry the spark of redemptive power in their lives. Our church is virtually ablaze with redemption!"

Perhaps it would help you to know that my story is similar in many respects to those in this book. I always believed in God, but thought of him as some distant person who was always watching me, just waiting to punish every wrong move I made. During my freshman year of college, I told a clergyman that I had a huge vacant spot in me, and I knew it wasn't homesickness. He suggested the remedy for me was to get involved in a church. I did, and I experienced a lot of religion, but I remained hollow inside. The empty feeling was there for the next ten years. I was just going through the motions of being in a church.

The turning point for me was the first face-to-face conversation I had with the woman who later became my wife. She asked me if I was a Christian. I answered "Yes," based on my church attendance, being a relatively "good" person, and the fact that I lived in America. Aren't we all Christians? From that day on, instead of church, I began hearing about relationship. This was different than any religion I had known. Then, late one night in a small Boise Chapel, I decided to quit trusting in my own efforts and myself. Over thirty years ago, at the age of twenty-eight, the emptiness that I could not fill up with *things*, was satisfied when I trusted the *person* of Jesus Christ.

My whole life changed—everything from leading a life of partying and playing, to my relationships with family and friends. Some didn't like the change because the old friendly, party guy didn't do the things he once did. Others saw the change, and were amazed at who I had become. When I found out that the God of the Bible is exactly who he says he is, I found my ticket to a whole new life.

If your life is in need of a radical change, as mine was, perhaps you would like to know more about this relationship with Jesus. Consider the following verses from the Bible:

Jesus spoke these words to his followers so that they could know how to fully experience the peace and the life that only he can give.

For God so loved the world that he gave his only Son, so that everyone who believes in him will not perish but have eternal life. John 3:16

Our problem is that we have all sinned and our sinful nature separates us from God.

156

Afterthoughts

For all have sinned; all fall short of God's glorious standard. Romans 3:23

We have tried to bridge the gap between God and man, but the only way to God is through Jesus, his Son.

For the wages of sin is death, but the free gift of God is eternal life through Christ Jesus our Lord. Romans 6:23

God expressed his love for us through the death and resurrection of his Son, Jesus. He paid the penalty for all of our sins and made a way for us to know his Father, God.

Jesus told him, "I am the way, the truth, and the life. No one can come to the Father except through me." John 14:6

We can choose to respond to Jesus' words by accepting the death and resurrection of Jesus as payment for our personal sins, and receiving him as our Savior and Lord.

But to all who believed him and accepted him, he gave the right to become children of God. John 1:12

Becoming a child of God is almost more wonderful than you can imagine. All it takes is repentance, which is turning away from our sins, and receiving Jesus Christ into our life by faith. In obedience, we choose to follow him as Lord of our lives. Does this mean we will never do wrong again? Not at all, but it does mean we can repent again, and ask for forgiveness. We can be confident that he hears us, and will wipe the slate clean again.

If you confess with your mouth that Jesus is Lord and believe in your heart that God raised him from the dead, you will be saved. Romans 10:9

If you want the ticket to this new life, it can be yours by praying a prayer like this:

Dear God, I know I am a sinner and the weight of guilt I carry with this sin is more than I can bear any longer. I repent and turn from my sins. I choose to believe that Jesus Christ died for my sins, he arose from the grave, and is alive forever. I open the door of my heart and life, and receive Jesus Christ as my Savior. I want to follow him and I make him Lord of my life. Thank you for my new life! Amen.

If you prayed that prayer, WELCOME to the family of God! You have an exciting new way of life ahead of you, and we would like to help you. Please call our office for more information, or tell us about your decision to follow Christ.

If you're looking for a church of genuine people with honest stories, we are located at 1177 N. Roosevelt Street in Boise. We would love to introduce you to the people in this book, whose stories you have just read.

Here's to YOUR new life!

Montie Ralstin

Boise Valley Christian Communion
1177 North Roosevelt
Boise, ID 83706

To find out more about us:
208-345-6776
Or visit us at:
www.BVCC.net

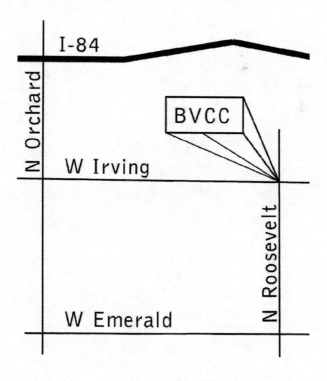

For more information on reaching your city with
stories from your church, please contact
Good Catch Publishing at…
www.goodcatchpublishing.com

GOOD CATCH
PUBLISHING